CFA INSTITUTE INDUSTRY GUIDES
THE REIT INDUSTRY

by Irfan Younus, CFA

ISBN 978-1-942713-08-1
April 2015

ABOUT THE AUTHOR

Irfan Younus, CFA, is an associate director in research and strategy at Cordea Savills LLP. He is responsible for producing economic and property market research for both his allocated markets and specialist sector, along with contributing to various publications, client presentations, and investment strategies. Prior to joining Cordea Savills, Mr. Younus worked at NCB (now part of Investec Group) as a sell-side analyst covering FTSE-listed real estate securities and at Barclays Investment Bank on its structured products team. He qualified as a Chartered Accountant at Ernst & Young in 2005, where he specialised in financial services, and is a member of the Chartered Institute for Securities & Investment.

CONTENTS

Industry Overview   **1**

    What Defines Real Estate?   3

    Real Estate as an Asset Class   3

    Means to Invest in Real Estate   5

What Is a Real Estate Investment Trust?   **9**

    How Does a Company Qualify as a REIT?   12

    Different Types of REITs   16

    Exploiting REIT Specialism as an Investment Strategy   20

    Who Manages a REIT?   20

    Key Features of a REIT   20

Key Terms   **24**

Financial Statement Analysis   **30**

    Equity REITs: Revenue   30

    Equity REITs: Expenses   32

    Equity REITs: Assets   34

    Equity REITs: Liabilities   34

    Mortgage REITs: Revenue   35

    Mortgage REITs: Expenses   36

    Mortgage REITs: Assets   36

    Mortgage REITs: Liabilities   38

Forecasting and Valuation   **39**

    Property Appraisals, Price Discovery, and the Concept of Smoothing   39

    Forecasting—Equity REITs   41

    Forecasting—Mortgage REITs   44

    How to Value a REIT   47

    What to Look for in a REIT   51

US and European REITs   **54**

Industry Resources   **75**

    Industry Journals   76

    Events and Conferences   77

INDUSTRY OVERVIEW

There is no getting away from real estate. We are all involved with it in one way or another. The delivery room of the hospital where we were born is real estate. The building that we call home is real estate. The place where we go to work every day is real estate. We farm on real estate, get married in it, and ultimately are buried in it. Real estate surrounds us.

Our society and its commercial activities are completely dependent on real estate and its natural resources for their existence.

The real estate industry is the largest single industry in the global economy. According to an estimate by Savills Research, the value of the world's real estate totalled approximately USD180 trillion at the end of 2013. Most of this amount represents directly owned residential property, of which 72% is owner occupied. Commercial property accounts for USD30 trillion.

Figure 1. Value of World's Real Estate, as of Year-End 2013

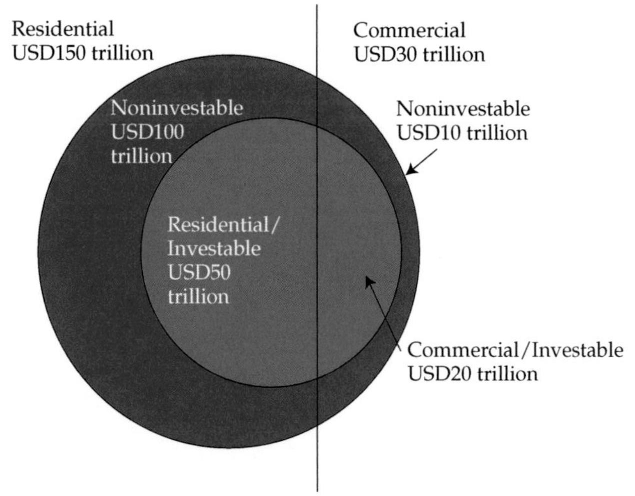

Source: Based on data from Savills Research.

The real estate market is split between investable real estate and noninvestable real estate. Investable real estate stock is defined as real estate that is owned for the primary purpose of benefitting from investment returns on those assets. Noninvestable stock includes real estate that is owner occupied or occupied by private and public companies, real estate owned by governments and used for governmental purposes, and residential buildings owned by private homeowners. The health care and education sectors are largely owner occupied, either by the public or private sector, although some properties in these industries are held for investment purposes and managed on that basis. Between the extremes of market size definition, with total stock on the one hand and professionally managed investment real estate on the other, there is a layer of a market strata that is considered as invested but not professionally managed. This layer relates to private individuals who may own a single property or a handful of smaller properties that are leased to others to gain an income stream and probably held in the expectation of future capital growth. In addition, there are organisations that own and lease real estate to tenants but whose primary objective is not the generation of an investment return. These include social housing organisations and municipalities, some of which have substantial real estate portfolios in a market. It is not uncommon in European countries for the social housing stock to be 20% of the total housing stock; the Netherlands, where social housing exceeds 30% of all housing by value, is a good example. All owner-occupied property has the potential to become investable in the future, but the probability of it becoming invested depends on the marketability of the stock and the willingness of the owner to sell its assets. **Table 1** shows the geographical breakdown of investment markets, their GDP, and their population.

Table 1. Geographical Breakdown of Investment Markets, GDP, and Population

	MSCI ACWI IM Index[1]	Commercial Real Estate Market Size[2]	GDP[2]	Population[2]
United States	52.4%	36.7%	22.2%	4.4%
Japan	7.5	11.6	6.5	1.8
United Kingdom	7.2	9.8	3.5	0.9
France	3.1	6.2	3.7	0.9
Canada	3.4	4.8	2.4	0.5
Germany	3.0	7.2	4.9	1.1
Other	23.4	23.7	56.7	90.4

Note: MSCI ACWI IM Index is MSCI's All Country World Index Investable Market Index.
[1]Data are as of February 2015.
[2]Data are as of 2013.
Sources: Based on data from MSCI, Investment Property Databank (IPD), the World Bank, and the Population Reference Bureau.

WHAT DEFINES REAL ESTATE?

Real estate is property consisting of land and anything fixed, immovable, or permanently attached to it, including buildings, fences, fixtures, infrastructure, or housing in general. The title to real estate normally includes the titles to air rights, mineral rights, and surface rights, which can be bought, leased, sold, or transferred together or separately.

REAL ESTATE AS AN ASSET CLASS

Real estate as an asset class has played a significant role in portfolios of private, commercial, and institutional investors. Real estate investments typically exhibit distinctive investment characteristics compared with conventional assets, such as stocks and bonds, particularly over long time periods.

Investments in real estate provide the potential for diversifying an investor's portfolio both for asset class allocations and geographic allocations. According to the National Association of Real Estate Investment Trusts (NAREIT), a study was performed in 2006 by Peter Westerheide that examined real estate investment trusts (REITs) and REIT-like securities in eight different countries, including the United States, Australia, and Japan. The findings were clear: "Real estate securities seem to represent an asset class distinct from bonds and stocks in most countries. In the long run, they seem to reflect the performance of direct real estate investments and provide a potential for further diversification of asset portfolios."[1] An examination of the correlation between different countries' real estate and equity markets from 1995 to 2013 (as shown in **Table 2** and **Table 3**) shows that the benefits of diversification appear stronger in real estate than in the traditional equity investment class.

Over longer time periods, commercial real estate investment has specific characteristics that help it keep pace with inflation. One of the key characteristics is the structure of a rental lease. Rent is usually negotiated when a lease is up for renewal. The rent on a shorter-term lease is likely to catch up to inflation more quickly than the rent on a longer-term lease, although longer-term leases often include step-ups in rent—sometimes explicitly tied to the inflation rate. The assignment of expenses can provide further insulation from inflation. For example, some leases allow property owners to pass through all expenses to their tenants.

Property values can be another important factor. When the economy is growing, interest rates generally rise, pushing property values down. At the same time, strengthening economic growth can increase net rental/operating income. The

---

[1]Peter Westerheide, "Cointegration of Real Estate Stocks and Reits with Common Stocks, Bonds and Consumer Price Inflation - An International Comparison," Discussion Paper No. 06-057, Centre for European Economic Research (August 2006), 4.

more net rental/operating income generated by a property in response to inflation, the greater the likelihood that the property will also appreciate in value, even if interest rates increase.

Table 2. Real Estate Market Correlations

	Australia	Canada	France	Ireland	Germany	Netherlands	New Zealand	UK	US
Australia	1.00								
Canada	0.90	1.00							
France	0.92	0.84	1.00						
Ireland	0.78	0.75	0.82	1.00					
Germany	−0.07	−0.03	−0.03	0.10	1.00				
Netherlands	0.58	0.47	0.78	0.73	0.11	1.00			
New Zealand	0.92	0.82	0.76	0.64	−0.36	0.36	1.00		
UK	0.55	0.51	0.54	0.74	−0.17	0.34	0.50	1.00	
US	0.87	0.91	0.77	0.76	0.14	0.46	0.72	0.61	1.00

Sources: Based on data from IPD and Cordea Savills.

Table 3. Equity Market Correlations

	Australia	Canada	France	Ireland	Germany	Netherlands	New Zealand	UK	US
Australia	1.00								
Canada	0.87	1.00							
France	0.83	0.87	1.00						
Ireland	0.61	0.47	0.73	1.00					
Germany	0.79	0.81	0.94	0.69	1.00				
Netherlands	0.86	0.81	0.94	0.73	0.91	1.00			
New Zealand	0.86	0.67	0.69	0.68	0.68	0.69	1.00		
UK	0.92	0.84	0.93	0.79	0.88	0.96	0.82	1.00	
US	0.74	0.79	0.87	0.74	0.86	0.88	0.70	0.90	1.00

Sources: Based on data from Bloomberg, MSCI indexes, and Cordea Savills.

These characteristics are stronger when the supply of real estate is limited. If local markets are building more space than their demand can absorb, the power to negotiate favourable lease terms, no matter what the inflation environment, shifts from owners to tenants. But no local market is exactly like another; supply conditions vary. Portfolio managers can exploit these differences to invest in markets that are less vulnerable to oversupply, thereby constructing portfolios with enhanced inflation protection.

Despite these well-recognised benefits of holding property in a multi-asset portfolio, institutional investors still appear to hold less property than anticipated by optimal portfolio theory; this underallocation can be attributed to the following reasons:

- Complexity of the operation of property holdings, including but not limited to illiquidity, lumpiness (large lot sizes), and depreciation

- Lack of confidence in available property data because of the possibility of smoothing in valuation-based indexes, which influences risk-adjusted performance and diversification

- Cyclicality in property returns, predominantly explained by inelasticity of property supply

As a consequence, property holdings in UK institutional portfolios have decreased from allocations as high as 15%–20% in the 1980s to less than 5% by the end of 2014.

MEANS TO INVEST IN REAL ESTATE

Compared with stocks and bonds, for which a single share or minimum number of units of a bond can be purchased, real estate assets are typically expensive. Only rarely will real estate investors pay the entire amount of the purchase price of a property in cash. Usually, a large portion of the purchase price is financed using some sort of financial instrument or debt, such as a mortgage loan collateralised by the property itself. The amount of the purchase price financed by debt is referred to as leverage. The amount financed by the investor's own capital, through cash or other asset transfers, is referred to as equity. But more often than not, an investor does not have enough cash to buy substantial real estate, such as office buildings. Therefore, equity is pooled together to form a collective investment scheme. In broad terms, investments in real estate can be made using the following methods:

- Direct property investment

- Unlisted real estate vehicles (open-end and closed-end funds)

- Listed real estate securities (including REITs and REOCs, or PropCos—real estate operating companies)

The main difference between open-end and closed-end funds is that in open-end funds, return of capital is arranged through the sale of units (redemption) to the manager, whereas in closed-end funds, return of capital occurs at the end of the life of the fund through the wind-up of the vehicle.

The two main features that distinguish REITs from other real estate operating companies are regulation and tax treatment. REOCs are subject to double taxation because profits are first taxed at the corporate level and then the post-tax dividends are taxed at the shareholders' level. REITs, in contrast, generally do not pay taxes on a company level and are exempt from capital gains tax upon disposal of the properties, provided that they distribute capital gains to their shareholders. If the REIT does not make such a distribution, then it must pay the tax.

The main advantages and disadvantages of different approaches to investing in real estate are summarised in **Table 4**.

Table 4. Advantages and Disadvantages of Different Approaches to Real Estate Investment

Investment Vehicle	Advantages	Disadvantages
Direct property	• Access to property returns • Ability to control both assets and management process	• Large lot size makes it unattainable for most investors • Diversification benefits only achievable within large portfolios • Low liquidity
Unlisted open-end funds	• Small lot size, thus the method is available to more investors • Diversification of market and specific risk • Higher liquidity provided through redemptions but subject to bid–offer spread or delay	• Lack of control • Slow expected cash drawdown often results in a conflict of interest between investors and managers • High manager and performance fees
Unlisted closed-end funds	• Diversification of market and specific risk • Professional and driven managers	• Initial performance distorted by costs of buying the portfolio • Low liquidity in closed-end funds
Listed property companies	• High liquidity • Small lot size: the problem of lumpiness is resolved through divisibility • Use of management skills	• Increased risk—volatility of share price (depends on anticipated asset value when compared with reported net asset value) • Double taxation (REITs are an exception)

Property, as with any other asset class, offers a wide range of investing opportunities depending on the investor's risk–return preferences. Real estate investment vehicles and unlisted real estate funds are typically classified by style as core, value added, or opportunistic.

- Core funds are low risk and have low leverage, often aiming to replicate the returns on a relevant index. Investments are made in "safe" markets, usually major metropolitan centres, in prime assets with secured long leases. The holding period is usually 7–15 years. Core funds offer medium to high liquidity.

- Value-added funds invest in more risky markets and assets but with the potential to generate higher returns. The typical strategy for a value-added fund is "buy-fix-sell", and a higher degree of leverage is allowed (50%–60%). Investments are allocated across all country types and across different sectors. Established as well as improving markets and primary and secondary cities are considered for investing. The holding period is usually 5–10 years, with low to medium liquidity.

- Opportunistic funds invest in the market and properties that exhibit the highest risk but are able to offer the highest returns. This type of fund typically has leverage levels of 60%–75%. The typical asset profile for an opportunistic fund is a distressed asset and development/redevelopment in secondary/tertiary locations. Consequently, liquidity is low and the holding periods are longer than five years.

Figure 2 shows the percentage allocation of real estate investment in these styles and REITs.

Figure 2. Allocations to Real Estate Investment Styles

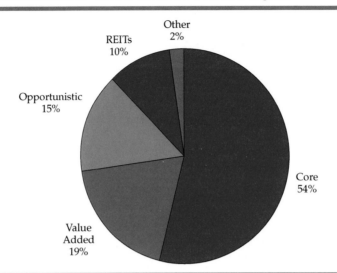

Notes: Percentages based on 138 asset owners in the survey universe. Calculation based on percentage of real assets in each category, not number of asset owners.
Sources: Based on data from IPD and MSCI.

WHAT IS A REAL ESTATE INVESTMENT TRUST?

Real estate investment trust is a term that originated in the United States and has since been adopted around the world to describe vehicles used for collective investments in real estate. REITs began under the Real Estate Investment Trust Act of 1960, part of the Cigar Excise Tax Extension Act of 1960, signed by President Dwight D. Eisenhower. REITs were created by the US Congress to give all investors the opportunity to invest in large-scale, diversified portfolios of income-producing real estate in the same way they typically invest in other asset classes.

During the early 1990s, REITs in the United States gained extensive recognition because they qualified to be an optimal vehicle enabling banks and the government to quickly liquidate nonperforming property and loan portfolios and helping to recapitalise the distressed property market. Subsequent creation of the umbrella partnership REIT (UPREIT) ensured the further explosive growth of securitisation through REITs because it allowed property owners to trade their assets for units in an operating partnership with capital gains tax payments deferred until the conversion of units into shares. As a result, the growth of the REIT market proved to be an essential driving force for improvement in property markets through the 1990s.

Since then, more than 38 countries around the world have established REIT regimes, with more countries in development. The spread of the REIT approach to real estate investment around the world has also increased awareness and acceptance of investing in global real estate securities.

In its essence, a REIT is a tax-efficient company that owns income-producing properties and can be generally classified into three main types: publicly listed, unlisted public, and (unlisted) private. This classification reflects the extent to which a REIT is subjected to analysis by public and regulatory requirements. Publicly listed REITs are the most transparent and visible, whereas unlisted REITs are less transparent to the public. Listed REITs can trade their securities on public markets, whereas unlisted REITs cannot trade on an open exchange and, consequently, are not liquid. REITs usually replicate the management style of a mutual fund and allow people to invest in property or mortgages on properties indirectly without actually buying the physical properties. The structure is designed to provide investors with a tax-efficient, low-cost, and immediate way of accessing the property market and, in particular, the rental income that the underlying assets generate. The net income (rental income after costs) is passed directly to shareholders in the form of dividends. Over time, dividends are likely to form an important proportion of the total return for shareholders.

Generally, REITs are exempt from paying corporate tax, but in return, they must distribute a significant majority of qualifying profits to shareholders as dividends (also known as property income distributions, or PIDs). (In the United States, REITs are subject to corporate income tax, but they can deduct distributions from taxable income. If they distribute at least 100% of taxable income, then they have no remaining tax liability.) The regulations on dividend payments imply that REITs' income returns are expected to closely approximate the income returns from property owned directly; thus, high compulsory distribution levels were designed to ensure that investors' risk is effectively paid off. As a result of high payouts, the taxation is moved from the corporate level to the investor level, and investors are liable for tax as if they held the property privately.

Today, REITs are globally recognised structures that exist around the world. The United States is by far the largest REIT market measured by market capitalisation of companies listed. The US market is followed by Australia, where 45 REITs represent 9.36% of the global REIT market. The introduction of REITs to Asia took place in the 1990s with the launch of Japanese REITs, which encouraged the development of REIT regimes in other Asian countries, particularly China, India, Malaysia, and South Korea. In Europe, the launch of a French REIT in 2003 triggered the later establishment of REIT markets in the United Kingdom and Germany in 2007 and 2008, respectively. Today, the United Kingdom is the fifth-largest REIT market globally. **Figure 3** shows the geographical mix of global REITs. For countries with REIT

Figure 3. Geographical Mix of Global REITs

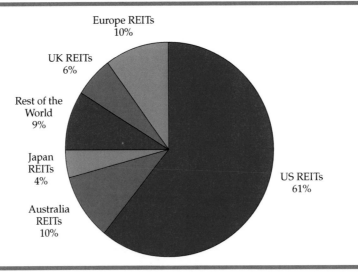

Sources: Based on data from British Land and the European Public Real Estate Association (EPRA).

regimes, **Table 5** lists the REIT structure, year enacted, number of REITs, sector market capitalisation, and percentage of global REITs.

Larger REITs are internally managed and will generally have their own internal property management operation, which helps to lower the overall cost of operations. Smaller REITs, in order to remain competitive, tend to develop a shared management platform in which the assets and strategic management are shared, usually with a sponsor, and the property management function is either internal or external to the REIT.

All REITs, whether open or closed, are governed by trust indentures and investment guidelines, which require the particular REIT to comply with requirements set out in the trust indenture and to follow the stated investment guidelines. These

Table 5.   Information about Global REIT Regimes

Country	REIT Structure	Year Enacted	Number of REITs	Sector Market Cap (USD millions)	Percentage of Global REIT
Australia	Listed Unit Trust	1985	45	71,764	9.36
Belgium	SICAFI	1995	17	8,917	0.83
Bulgaria	SPIC	2004	22	395	0.04
Finland	FINNISH REIT	2009	—	—	—
France	SIIC	2003	37	68,193	6.33
Germany	G-REIT	2007	4	1,657	0.15
Greece	REIC	1999	3	637	0.06
Hong Kong	HK-REIT	2003	11	23,925	2.22
Ireland	REIT	2013	1	472	0.04
Israel	REIT	2006	—	—	—
Italy	SIIQ	2007	2	1,602	0.15
Lithuania	REIT	2008	—	—	—
Luxembourg	REIT	2007	—	—	—
Netherlands	FBI	1969	5	8,745	0.81
Spain	SOCIMI	2009	—	—	—
Turkey	REIC	2013	25	8,237	0.76
United Kingdom	UK-REIT	2007	23	49,007	4.55
United States	US-REIT	1960	163	621,294	54.68

Source: Based on data from EPRA as of June 2014.

requirements are set by the local legislation authority for the sector to qualify for favourable tax treatment. The trust indenture covers such matters as payment of distributions and limitations on the REIT's borrowing capacity.

HOW DOES A COMPANY QUALIFY AS A REIT?

It is important to understand that investment companies and groups elect to become REITs; it is not forced on them. Depending on local law, guidelines, and regulations, qualifying REIT companies have the following characteristics.

- They must meet certain conditions, including minimum levels of interest cover and the proportion of total profits and assets that relate to their property rental businesses.

- They are not required to pay corporate tax on profits and gains from their qualifying property rental business. Note that the tax benefits of REITs only apply to the qualifying investment activity of the REIT—that is, investment in real estate to derive income after complying with conditions implemented by the local regulatory authorities. **Table 6** details some of these conditions. Non-qualifying activities—for example, in the United Kingdom, where property trading activity is more than 25%—will be taxed as per normal corporate tax. Companies that have a mixture of trading and investment activity will need to divest themselves of at least part of their non-property-holding businesses in order to qualify for REIT status. The most likely means of restructuring is to demerge the two activities. The shareholders would still retain an interest in the other trading activities, but these would be carried out through a different company than before, whereas the property would be held by an investment company that could convert to a REIT. Property development is not prohibited within a REIT, but to the extent that the activity is taxed as a trade, the income and gains will be in the non-ring-fenced business (i.e., will fall outside the REIT's regime). This non-ring-fenced business must not breach income and asset limits set by the local authority.

- They are required to distribute to shareholders a significant amount of the profits arising from the tax-exempt business, normally within one year from the end of the accounting period concerned. The distribution ratio, depending on different geographic requirements, varies between 75% and 100%.

- They are not required to distribute tax-exempt capital gains on the sale of investment properties. But if the REIT does not distribute capital gains to shareholders, then it must pay capital gains tax.

- They are managed by a board of directors or trustees.

- They have a minimum number of shares depending on different geographic requirements.

- They have shares that are fully transferable.

- They are subject to local regulation and can have no more than 50% of their shares held by five or fewer individuals during the last half of the taxable year.

- They invest at least 75% of their total assets in real estate assets.

- They derive at least 75% of their gross income from rents from real property or interest on mortgages financing real property.

Table 6. Examples of REIT Regime Requirements around the World

Country	Legal Form	Minimum Share Capital	Shareholder Requirements	Maximum Leverage	Minimum Profit Distribution Obligations
Australia	Unit trust	—	—	Unlimited, but interest deduction restrictions	—
Belgium	Resident joint stock company or partnership	EUR1.25 million	—	65%	80%
Bulgaria	Joint stock company	EUR255,646	30% of institutional investor	20%	90%
Finland	Public limited company	EUR5 million	One shareholder cannot own 10% or more of the total share capital	80%	90%
France	Joint stock company or partnership (limited by shares)	EUR15 million	One shareholder cannot own more than 60% of the share capital	50%	85%

(continued)

Table 6. Examples of REIT Regime Requirements around the World (continued)

Country	Legal Form	Minimum Share Capital	Shareholder Requirements	Maximum Leverage	Minimum Profit Distribution Obligations
Germany	Joint stock company	EUR15 million	15% of shares must be widely held; one shareholder cannot own more than 10% of the voting rights	45%	90%
Greece	Listed société anonyme	EUR25 million	—	75%	50%
Hong Kong	Unit trust	—	—	45%	90%
Ireland	Irish incorporated company	EUR38,092	One shareholder cannot own 10% or more of the total share capital	Financing ratio of at least 1.25:1	85%
Israel	Public company traded on the Tel Aviv Stock Exchange	—	At least 50% of the company's means of control are held by more than five shareholders	60%	90%
Italy	Joint stock company	EUR40 million	One shareholder cannot own 50% or more of the total share capital	Restrictions set by company bylaws	85%
Lithuania	Joint stock company	EUR43,500	—	75%	—
Luxembourg	Fonds commun de placement, Société d'investissement à capital variable, Société d'Investissement à Capital Fixe	EUR1.25 million	—	—	—

(continued)

Table 6. Examples of REIT Regime Requirements around the World (continued)

Country	Legal Form	Minimum Share Capital	Shareholder Requirements	Maximum Leverage	Minimum Profit Distribution Obligations
Netherlands	Naamloze Vennootschap, Besloten Vennootschap, Fondsen voor gemene rekening, or comparable foreign entity	EUR45,000	One shareholder cannot own 25% or more of the total share capital for listed company, 5% for not listed	60%	100%
Spain	Joint stock company	EUR5 million	—	—	100%
Turkey	Joint stock company	TRY30 million	—	Short-term credits limited to five times the net asset value	20%
United Kingdom	Listed closed-end company	GBP50,000	One shareholder cannot own 10% or more of the total share capital	Interest cover test	90%
United States	Legal US domestic entity	—	At least 100 shareholders with no one controlling more than 50% of shares	—	90%

Source: Based on information from EPRA.

DIFFERENT TYPES OF REITS

The REIT industry has a diverse profile, which offers many investment opportunities. However, REITs are often classified as either equity or mortgage.

■ Equity REITs mostly own and operate income-producing real estate. They have increasingly become real estate operating companies engaged in a wide range of real estate activities, including leasing, maintenance, and development of real property, as well as tenant services. One major distinction between equity REITs and other real estate companies is that an equity REIT must acquire and develop its properties primarily to operate them as part of its own portfolio rather than to resell them once they are developed.

■ REITs can either invest in a wide range of real estate (known as diversified REITs) or specialise in one sector. Specialism in an individual sector allows a REIT to focus on one sector and develop better technical ability for that sector. Although it remains to be determined which strategy outperforms in the long run, diversified REITs have previously justified their diversification by claiming that they have the opportunity to take advantage of timing differences between property subsector cycles. The rationale is that the opportunity cost of specialisation outweighs its benefits.

■ REITs own and manage a variety of property types: shopping centres, health care facilities, apartments, warehouses, office buildings, hotels, and others. **Table 7** lists characteristics of various commercial real estate sectors. Most REITs specialise in only one property type, such as shopping malls, timberlands, data centres, or self-storage facilities. According to the Global Industry Classification Standard, as published by MSCI, there are nine subindustries of REITs:

1. *Diversified REITs.* Companies or trusts with diversified operations across two or more property types

2. *Industrial REITs.* Companies or trusts engaged in the acquisition, development, ownership, leasing, management, and operation of industrial properties, including companies operating industrial warehouses and distribution properties

3. *Hotel and resort REITs.* Companies or trusts engaged in the acquisition, development, ownership, leasing, management, and operation of hotel and resort properties

4. *Office REITs.* Companies or trusts engaged in the acquisition, development, ownership, leasing, management, and operation of office properties

Table 7. Characteristics of Commercial Real Estate Sectors

Property Sector	Economic Drivers	Lease Duration	Construction Cycle	Relative Cyclicality
Hotel	The main drivers of the hotel sector are business and consumer sentiment, corporate profitability, and transportation costs.	1 day	2 years	Very high
	Hotels are highly cyclical as a result of their nightly leases because room rates and occupancies can change swiftly with economic conditions. Low relative operating margins and significant recurring capital expenditure add volatility to the cash flow profile.			
Self-storage	The main drivers of the self-storage sector are employment growth (particularly in urban areas where space is more limited), housing transactions, and household size.	1 month	6 months	High
	Lease terms are relatively short, but self-storage companies have strong pricing power because small businesses and apartment dwellers will typically agree to higher rents rather than discard belongings or move into a larger space.			
Apartment	The main drivers of the apartment sector are population, household formation, job growth, home affordability, and sentiment towards owning a property.	1 year	1–1.5 years	High to medium
	Apartment REITs are largely cyclical because profitability is tied to employment rates. But they tend to be inversely (negatively) correlated with residential housing (tighter mortgage requirements and uncertainty on home prices tend to benefit apartment demand).			
Shopping centre	The main drivers of the shopping centre sector are consumer spending, disposable income, e-commerce trends, and employment.	3–5 years	12 months	Low to medium
	Tenants are generally geared towards nondiscretionary spending (grocery, discount retail, pharmacy), offering some defensive qualities. Big box centres generally have stronger-credit tenants but are also at greater risk from e-commerce penetration. Neighbourhood centres typically include more local businesses (nail salons, pizza parlours), which are more dependent on the local economy.			

(continued)

Table 7. Characteristics of Commercial Real Estate Sectors (continued)

Property Sector	Economic Drivers	Lease Duration	Construction Cycle	Relative Cyclicality
Industrial	The main drivers of the industrial sector are manufacturing, logistics, exports, shipping volumes, and business sentiment.	3–6 years	6 months	Medium
	Despite long lease durations, industrial properties have short construction times because of less-complex building requirements, so supply tends to closely track demand. A shorter property cycle results in greater sensitivity to domestic and global economic growth.			
Regional shopping centre	The main drivers of the regional shopping centre sector are the local economy, proximity to other villages and towns, consumer sentiment, and house prices.	5–10 years	1.5–2 years	Low
	Tenants tend to be focused on discretionary spending (department stores, boutique retail). Leases typically include rent step-ups, providing some support in the event of a downturn in the economy.			
Office	The main drivers of the office sector are corporate profits, employment growth, the economy, and business outlook.	5–10 years	1.5–2 years	Low to medium
	Lengthy lease durations (10 years or more for urban offices) provide long-term cash flow visibility. Offices in central business districts often see near-constant low supply conditions.			
Health care	The main drivers of the health care sector are the government's commitment to health care spending, insurance rates, and an aging population.	8–10+ years	1–1.5 years	Very low to medium
	Long-term tenants, such as hospitals and medical office buildings, provide generally stable, bond-like income payments, resulting in a defensive investment profile.			

Sources: Based on information from NAREIT and Cordea Savills.

5. *Health care REITs.* Companies or trusts engaged in the acquisition, development, ownership, leasing, management, and operation of properties serving the health care industry, including hospitals, nursing homes, and assisted living properties

6. *Residential REITs.* Companies or trusts engaged in the acquisition, development, ownership, leasing, management, and operation of residential properties, including multifamily homes, apartments, manufactured homes, and student housing properties

7. *Retail REITs.* Companies or trusts engaged in the acquisition, development, ownership, leasing, management, and operation of shopping malls, outlet malls, and neighbourhood/community shopping centres

8. *Specialised REITs.* Companies or trusts engaged in the acquisition, development, ownership, leasing, management, and operation of properties not classified elsewhere. This subindustry includes trusts that operate and invest in storage properties as well as REITs that do not generate a majority of their revenues and income from real estate rental and leasing operations.

9. *Mortgage REITs.* Mortgage REITs mostly lend money directly to real estate owners and operators or extend credit indirectly through the acquisition of loans or mortgage-backed securities. Today's mortgage REITs generally extend mortgage credit only on existing properties. Many mortgage REITs also manage their interest rate and credit risks using securitised mortgage investments, dynamic hedging techniques, and other accepted derivative strategies.

■ Hybrid REITs have investments in both direct real estate and mortgage-backed securities.

■ Stapled securities are a variation of hybrid structures. These REITs provide investors with exposure to a fund management and/or a property development company, as well as a real estate portfolio. A share in a stapled securities fund usually consists of one trust unit and one share in the fund management company. These securities are "stapled" and cannot be traded separately. The trust holds the portfolio of assets, whereas the related company carries out the fund's management functions and/or manages any development opportunities.

EXPLOITING REIT SPECIALISM AS AN INVESTMENT STRATEGY

Companies generally sell more goods and services early in an economic recovery and, therefore, employ more people. As companies grow, they need to take on more space, which benefits office and industrial REITs. As more people join the work force, they initially pay down excess debt, and with disposable income rising, individuals tend to spend more in retail shopping outlets and on travel, which benefits retail REITs as well as hotel and resort REITs. Because improving economies and employment generally increase the demand for housing, both the owner-occupied housing market and residential REITs may benefit at the same time. Some of this housing-related activity may be curtailed by an increase in the cost of credit associated with rising interest/mortgage rates, which might hurt home purchasing activity while potentially helping apartment rentals. Improved activity in the housing market supports relocation, which benefits self-storage REITs. With an aging population, health care REITs are usually considered defensive investments.

WHO MANAGES A REIT?

Similar to other publicly traded companies, a REIT's executive management team operates the company, deciding what properties it will own and manage. Management decisions are overseen by a board of directors that is responsible to the shareholders. As with other corporations, REIT directors are typically well-known and respected members of the real estate, business, and professional communities. Many of today's REITs became public companies within the past 20–25 years, often transforming to public ownership what previously had been private enterprises. In many cases, the majority owners of these private enterprises became the senior officers of the REIT and contributed their ownership positions to the REIT.

KEY FEATURES OF A REIT

The following are some of the key features of a REIT.

- *High yield through regular distributions.* As highlighted previously, a REIT indenture typically contains a clause that requires a REIT to distribute a significant percentage of its distributable income to its unitholders. Every REIT defines how it calculates its distributable income. Different geographic jurisdictions have different distribution limits. On average, between 75% and 100% of distributable income is distributed to unitholders. Distributions from REITs are taxed differently from dividends from non-REIT companies (or corporations).

- *Taxation.* Another feature that makes a REIT attractive to investors is the favourable tax treatment of income earned within a REIT, as well as the fact that unitholders can partially manage their own tax affairs. The REIT's taxable income is initially determined in a similar manner as that of a corporation. As long as 100% of the taxable income of the REIT is allocated to its unitholders, it will not be subject to tax.

- *Focused real estate subsegment exposure.* Different REITs can have a different strategic focus in regard to which types of assets they want to hold in their portfolios. This feature allows investors to focus on a specific segment of properties within the real estate industry.

- *Volatility.* REITs have exhibited lower volatility when compared with other equity sectors. The main reason is the fact that they generate contractual revenues and are able to maintain a high yield during short-term economic conditions compared with other equities that are more susceptible to market volatility. But REITs are part of the stock market, and both their share price and their capital returns are greatly affected by that market. Accordingly, they have a higher volatility of returns, particularly when compared with private real estate.

- *Secondary offerings.* A secondary offering is the issuance of new stock for public sale from a company that has already made its initial public offering. REITs are known to issue secondary offerings more often than other equity classes. The main reason is that REITs distribute much of their income, which results in a lack of retained and redeployable capital. As a result, many REITs often choose to place secondary offerings to raise capital and increase market valuation. But such actions are often dilutive and thus potentially negative for equityholders.

- *Property development.* Another way for a REIT to grow its equity is through developments. Although the extent of development that a REIT can under-take is limited by local REIT regulations, REITs often take advantage of the property cycle and ramp up their development pipelines during early stages of an economic recovery.

- *Liquidity.* Shares of publicly traded REITs are readily converted into cash because they trade on the major stock exchanges. This feature is a sig-nificant benefit compared with selling a property outright, which could take months to complete and realise a return. Conversely, unlisted REITs cannot be sold easily. An investor who is forced to sell can expect to take a significant loss.

■ *Returns.* Evidence from academic research suggests that in the short term (up to five years), REITs and real property show largely different returns. But in the long term (10 years and more), REITs and real property on average produce the same returns.[2]

■ *Professional managers.* REIT managers are skilled, experienced real estate professionals.

■ *Transparency.* Public REITs are required to disclose detailed information about their holdings, executive compensation, and other aspects of their business. This requirement provides more transparency relative to other types of property investments. However, it is worth noting that unlisted REITs have a chequered history of transparency and disclosure to their investors. For example, some unlisted REITs have promised an appealing annual yield, but to meet those yield targets, they borrowed money or returned some of the investors' original capital, which creates an illusion of an investment with higher yield than what is actually achievable based on the underlying investments.

■ *Diversification benefits.* In a multi-asset portfolio, REITs tend to act more like return enhancers than risk diversifiers. Over longer periods, however, REITs mimic the features of direct real estate investment and their inclusion in a portfolio as a substitution for private property might be justified. In addition, REITs offer global diversification opportunities for investors both in terms of underlying returns and access to experienced local management teams.

■ *Market access.* Public REITs have a tendency to purchase the best properties in the largest markets. These "Class A" properties are pricey and tend to offer lower yields because many other REITs, pension funds, and even sovereign wealth funds aim to purchase only these "trophy" properties. In contrast, unlisted REITs have historically purchased "Class B" properties in secondary markets. To the extent that there is less competition for these properties,

---

[2]See the following:

S. Michael Giliberto, "Equity Real Estate Investment Trusts and Real Estate Returns," *Journal of Real Estate Research*, vol. 5, no. 2 (February 1990): 259–264.

David M. Geltner and Brian Kluger, "REIT-Based Pure Play Portfolios: The Case of Property Types," *Real Estate Economics*, vol. 26, no. 4 (December 1998): 581–612.

Gregory H. MacKinnon and Ashraf Al Zaman, "Real Estate for the Long Term: The Effect of Return Predictability on Long-Horizon Allocations," *Real Estate Economics*, vol. 37, no. 1 (Spring 2009): 117–153.

Elias Oikarinen, Martin Hoesli, and Camilo Serrano, "The Long-Run Dynamics between Direct and Securitized Real Estate," *Journal of Real Estate Research*, vol. 33, no. 1 (2011): 73–104.

they can offer higher yields and give investors exposure to a different type of property than public REITs generally provide.

■ *Scale.* Most of the largest REITs are public. These firms enjoy some economies of scale and better diversification and will generally attract top human resource talent.

KEY TERMS

Real estate is a specialised sector with its own key terms and metrics. It is useful to understand them before analysing the financials of property securities or valuing them. The following are some of the key terms.

- *Adjusted funds from operations (AFFO).* This term refers to a computation that measures a real estate company's operational cash flow. AFFO is considered to be a more accurate measure of economic income than funds from operations (FFO). It is calculated by adjusting FFO to remove any noncash rent that has been recognised and subtracting maintenance-type capital expenditures and leasing costs (including leasing agents' commissions and tenants' improvement allowances).

- *ARES.* The Association for Real Estate Securitization is a Japan-based association seeking to expand the range of investment opportunities available to institutional and individual investors.

- *Capitalisation rate.* The capitalisation rate (or cap rate) for a property is determined by dividing the property's net operating income by its purchase price. Generally, high cap rates indicate higher returns and greater perceived risk.

- *Capped rents* are subject to a maximum level of uplift at the specified rent review as agreed to at the time of leasing. *Collar rents* are subject to a minimum level of uplift at the specified rent review as agreed to at the time of leasing.

- *Cash (or funds) available for distribution:* CAD (or FAD) is a measure of a REIT's ability to generate cash and to distribute dividends to its shareholders. In addition to subtracting from FFO normalised recurring real estate–related expenditures and other noncash items to obtain AFFO, CAD (or FAD) is usually derived by subtracting nonrecurring expenditures.

- *Commercial mortgage-backed securities (CMBS).* CMBS are a type of mortgage-backed security backed by commercial mortgages rather than residential real estate. CMBS issues are usually structured as multiple tranches, similar to collateralised mortgage obligations (CMOs), rather than typical residential "pass-throughs."

- *DownREIT.* A DownREIT structure is an expansion of an existing REIT structure that forms a new partnership to acquire and own property. The term "DownREIT" refers to a REIT that owns properties directly but also holds some of its properties in a partnership. Owners of a DownREIT hold their interests as operating units (OP units) in the partnership until they are redeemed or exchanged for cash or REIT shares. In most cases, no tax liability is triggered when the owner/developer contributes properties to the operating partnership. The owner/developer's units become taxable when the partnership units are converted into stock or the partnership assets are sold. In a DownREIT structure, the REIT becomes the general partner and the economic interests of the other partners are aligned with the management and stockholders of the REIT. In most cases, distributions to OP unitholders closely track the dividends paid by the REIT to its shareholders. Properties held in the DownREIT partnership will benefit from the REIT's management expertise and cash contributions to discharge debt or improve the properties.

- *Estimated rental value (ERV)*. ERV is the open market rent that a property can be reasonably expected to attain given its characteristics, condition, location, and local market conditions. ERV is often compared with passing rent, which is the current rent paid to the landlord. Such comparisons are done to adjust rental rates when a lease is up for renewal.

- *EPRA*. The European Public Real Estate Association is the industry body for European REITs.

- *Equitisation*. Equitisation is the process by which the economic benefits of ownership of a tangible asset, such as real estate, are divided among numerous investors and represented in the form of publicly traded securities.

- *Equity REIT*. An equity REIT is one that owns, or has an equity interest in, rental real estate (rather than making loans secured by real estate collateral).

- *Funds from operations (FFO)*: FFO is the most commonly accepted and reported measure of REIT operating performance. It is equal to a REIT's net income, excluding gains or losses from sales of property, plus real estate depreciation.

- *Gross rental income (also see straight lining)*. The gross accounting rent receivable (quoted either for the period or on an annualised basis) prepared under International Financial Reporting Standards that requires that rental income from fixed/minimum guaranteed rent reviews and tenant incentives is spread on a straight-line basis over the entire lease to first break. This approach can result in income being recognised ahead of cash flow.

- *Hybrid REIT*. A hybrid REIT is one that combines the investment strategies of both equity REITs and mortgage REITs.

- *Interest coverage.* Interest coverage is the number of times net interest payable is covered by underlying profit before net interest payable and taxation.

- *Lease incentives.* Lease incentives are offered to a prospective tenant to enter into a lease. The value of the lease incentive is spread over the noncancellable life of the lease.

- *Leasing and lease renewals.* Renewals are generally classified as either short term (less than two years) or long term (more than two years). Leasing and renewals are compared with both the previous passing rent as of the start of the financial year and the ERV immediately prior to leasing. Both comparisons are made on a net effective basis.

- *Loan-to-value (LTV).* LTV is the ratio of the principal value of gross debt less cash, short-term deposits, and liquid investments to the aggregate value of properties and investments.

- *Mark to market.* Mark to market is the process of recording the price of an asset or liability to reflect its current market value.

- *Mortgage REIT.* A mortgage REIT is one that makes or owns loans and other obligations that are secured by real estate collateral.

- *NAREIT.* The National Association of Real Estate Investment Trusts is an association representing publicly traded real estate companies with an interest in US real estate and capital markets.

- *Net asset value (NAV).* NAV is the net market value of a company's assets, including but not limited to its properties, after subtracting all its liabilities and obligations.

- *Net development value.* Net development value is the estimated end value of a development project as determined by external valuers for when the building is completed and fully leased (taking into account tenant incentives and notional purchaser's costs). It is based on the appraiser's view on ERVs, yields, vacancies, and rent-free periods.

- *Net effective rent.* Net effective rent is the contracted gross rent receivable, taking into account any rent-free period or other tenant incentives. The incentives are treated as a cost to rent and spread over the lease to the earliest termination date.

- *Net equivalent yield.* Net equivalent yield is the weighted-average income return (after allowing for notional purchaser's costs) a property will produce based on the timing of the income received. In accordance with usual practice, the equivalent yields (as determined by the external valuers) assume rent is received annually in arrears.

- *Net initial yield.* Net initial yield is the current annualised rent, net of costs, expressed as a percentage of capital value after allowing for notional purchaser's costs.

- *Net rental income.* Net rental income is the rental income receivable in the period after payment of direct property outgoings that typically comprise ground rents payable under head leases, vacancy costs, net service charge expenses, and other direct irrecoverable property expenses. Net rental income is quoted on an accounting basis. It will differ from annualised net cash rents and passing rent because of the effects of income from rent reviews, net property outgoings, and accounting adjustments for fixed and minimum contracted rent reviews and lease incentives.

- *Net reversionary yield.* Net reversionary yield is the anticipated yield to which the initial yield will rise (or fall) once the rent reaches the estimated rental value.

- *Occupancy rate.* Occupancy rate is the estimated rental value of leased units as a percentage of the total estimated rental value of the portfolio, excluding development properties. It includes accommodations under offer or subject to asset management (meaning they have been taken back for refurbishment and are not available to lease as of the balance sheet date).

- *Over rented.* The term is used to describe when the contracted rent is more than the estimated rental value.

- *Overall "topped-up" net initial yield.* The annual net rents on investment properties are expressed as a percentage of the investment property valuation after adding purchasers' costs.

- *Passing rent.* Passing rent is the gross rent less any ground rent payable under head leases.

- *Portfolio valuation movement.* Portfolio valuation movement is the increase in value of the portfolio of properties held as of the balance sheet date and net sales receipts of those sold during the period, expressed as a percentage of the capital value at the start of the period plus net capital expenditure, capitalised interest, and transaction costs.

- *Positive spread investing (PSI).* PSI is the ability to raise funds (both equity and debt) at a cost significantly lower than the initial returns that can be obtained on real estate transactions.

- *Property income distributions.* Property income distributions are profits distributed to shareholders that are subject to tax as property income.

- *Rack-rented.* The term is used to describe when the contracted rent is in line with the estimated rental value, implying a nil reversion.

- *REIA.* The Real Estate Institute of Australia is the national professional association for Australia's real estate sector.

- *Rent reviews.* These reviews take place at intervals agreed to in the lease (typically every five years), and their purpose is to adjust the rent to the current market level at the review date. For upward-only rent reviews, the rent will either remain at the same level or increase (if market rents have increased) at the review date.

- *Residential mortgage-backed securities (RMBS).* RMBS are mortgage-backed securities that are supported by cash payments received from homeowners who pay interest and principal according to terms agreed to with their lenders. In the United States, depending on whether it is an agency mortgage-backed security (MBS) or a nonagency MBS, RMBS may be issued by structures set up by government-sponsored enterprises, such as Fannie Mae or Freddie Mac, or they can be "private label", which are issued by structures set up by investment banks.

- *Securitisation.* Securitisation is the process of financing a pool of similar but unrelated financial assets (usually loans or other debt instruments) by issuing to investors security interests that represent claims against the cash flow and other economic benefits generated by the pool of assets.

- *Straight lining.* Straight-line rent is the concept that the total liability under a rental lease should be charged as an expense on an even basis over the term of the lease. The concept is similar to straight-line depreciation, whereby the cost of an asset is charged to expense on an even basis over the useful life of the asset. The straight-line concept is based on the idea that the usage of a lease is consistent over time; that is, the leased asset is used at about the same rate from month to month. To calculate straight-line rent, aggregate the total cost of all lease payments and divide by the total lease term. The result is the amount to be charged to expense in each month of the lease. This calculation should include all discounts from the normal rent, as well as extra charges that can reasonably be expected to be incurred over the life of the lease.

- *Umbrella partnership REIT (UPREIT).* In a typical UPREIT, the partners of the existing partnerships and a newly formed REIT become partners in a new partnership called an "operating partnership". For their respective interests in the operating partnership, the partners contribute the properties from the existing partnership and the REIT contributes the cash proceeds from its public offering. The REIT typically is the general partner and the majority owner of the operating partnership units.

FINANCIAL STATEMENT ANALYSIS

The structure of a REIT's financial statements varies with the type of REIT. An equity REIT derives most of its income from the rental income of properties it owns. A mortgage REIT derives most of its income from interest it receives on mortgage-backed securities. Similarly, an increase in the NAVs of equity REITs depends on compression or softening cap values, but the mortgage REIT's asset values depend on the interest rate curve and mortgage mortality rates.

The following are key financial statement components relevant for financial statement analysis of equity REITs and mortgage REITs.

EQUITY REITS: REVENUE

Rental income represents the primary source of income for equity REITs. This rental income is receivable in the period after payment of direct property outgoings, which typically comprise ground rents payable under head leases, vacancy costs, net service charge expenses, and other direct irrecoverable property expenses. Net rental income is quoted on an accounting basis, meaning that it will differ from annualised net cash rents and passing rent because of the effects of income from rent reviews, net property outgoings, and accounting adjustments for fixed and minimum contracted rent reviews and lease incentives.

Rent leases are usually agreed to for a fixed number of years, and during the agreed-on term, open market rents may differ from what the tenant is paying. This factor can impact the value of the underlying asset. A shorter lease term increases the potential for a vacancy risk in the future, and therefore, property valuers tend to assign lower property values. An exception to this possibility is if the asset is located in a prime location (e.g., retail shop in Times Square in New York City, retail shop in Oxford Street in London).

It is important to understand the variations in lease types. Broadly, there are four types of leases.

- *Single net lease.* In a single net lease, the tenant is responsible for paying property taxes. Single net leases are less than double or triple net leases because all or the majority of the expenses are passed on to the tenant.

- *Double net lease.* In a double net lease, the tenant is responsible for property tax and building insurance. The landlord is responsible for any expenses incurred for structural repairs and common area maintenance.

- *Triple net lease.* A triple net lease (or net-net-net lease) is a lease agreement in which the tenant agrees to pay all real estate taxes, building insurance, and maintenance (the three "nets") on the property in addition to any normal fees that are expected under the agreement (rent, utilities, etc.). In such a lease, the tenant is responsible for all costs associated with the repair and maintenance of any common area. An extreme variation of a triple net lease is a bondable lease (true triple net lease or absolute triple net lease), whereby the tenant carries every imaginable real estate risk related to the property. Notably, these additional risks include the obligations to rebuild after a casualty, regardless of the adequacy of insurance proceeds, and to pay rent after partial or full condemnation. These leases are not terminable by the tenant, nor are rent abatements permissible. The concept is to make the rent absolutely net under all circumstances, equivalent to the obligations of a bond.

- *Ground lease.* A ground lease is another variation of a net lease. Under a ground lease, the landowner leases the land to the lessee, which gives the lessee the opportunity to construct a building. The lessee will then have a leasehold interest in the property. Under a ground lease, the tenant will typically pay for the same items as under a triple net lease or bondable lease. Generally, ownership of the building will revert to the landowner at conclusion of the lease.

The open market rent, or ERV, is a rent that a property can be reasonably expected to attain given its characteristics, condition, location, and local market conditions. ERV is often compared with passing rent, which is current rent paid to the landlord. Such comparisons are done to adjust rental rates when a lease is up for renewal. In an undersupplied rental market, in which demand for properties exceeds supply, the vacancy rate is decreasing, and rents are rising, the ERV may exceed the passing rent. Hence, the landlord is no longer maximising the rental revenue from the lease. However, an analyst can ascertain the gap between passing rent and ERV to forecast future uplifts, which, given the cap rate, translates into higher property value. Similarly, in an oversupplied market, in which supply of properties exceeds demand, the vacancy rate is increasing, and rents are declining, the ERV will be lower. Here the landlord is maximising the rental revenue from the lease but at a greater likelihood of vacancy on expiration of the lease. Analysts should also look at cues for the change in like-for-like ERV growth on the standing investment properties over the reporting period and like-for-like rental income growth on properties owned throughout the current and previous periods under review to ascertain and project future rental income. This figure is then adjusted with incentives and rent-free periods to arrive at cash rental income.

A REIT that relies on a handful of tenants will face greater vacancy risks than a REIT that draws its income from a diversified pool of tenants. For example, **Table 8** shows the breakdown by tenant and industry of properties in British Land's portfolio. A lease expiration profile by tenant will flag those renters at risk of not renewing their leases. Sometimes, the REIT may be performing well as a whole but the existence of certain underperforming properties may drag its overall figures down. A lease expiration profile by portfolio will flag the specific properties that may be a challenge, especially properties with very short lease terms.

Analysts should also look at vacancies and discuss with management the steps to be taken to mitigate the vacant space. Vacancy can have multiple negative effects: it reduces income, appraisers usually assign higher cap rates for a vacant space and thus lower asset values, and in some countries, landlords have to pay business rates or taxes on vacant commercial properties. Analysts should also compare a REIT's vacancy rate with market vacancy rates for the relevant subsegment. If assets are not obsolete for the purpose of their use, a lower market vacancy rate and a higher net absorption rate suggest that a REIT should be able to find tenants quickly. This analysis will allow for a determination as to whether rolling tenant rates will roll up or down.

Another revenue item that appears on the income statement is the valuation movement and realised surpluses or deficits arising from the property investment and development portfolio. Analysts should make a note that REIT legislation on property development varies across geographic areas. Although it is not prohibited, the activity can be taxed differently. But if executed properly, it reaps a much higher return on equity invested.

It is worth highlighting that a number of steps have been taken by various professional bodies on the convergence of valuation definitions across geographies and professional bodies. Analysts should review local valuation standards to do an accurate like-for-like comparison.

EQUITY REITS: EXPENSES

Net overhead and operating expenses relate to all administrative expenses, including the share of joint ventures' overhead and operating expenses, net of any service fees, recharges, or other income specifically intended to cover overhead and property expenses. The EPRA recommends use of the EPRA cost ratio, a ratio of net overhead and operating expenses to gross rental income (with both amounts excluding ground rents payable) to compare operating expenses across the sector.

Adjusted earnings is the profit after taxation, excluding investment and development property revaluations and gains/losses on disposals, changes in the fair value of financial instruments, and associated closeout costs and their related taxation.

Table 8. Breakdown by Tenant and Industry of British Land Properties, as of 30 September 2014

	Percentage of Contracted Rent
Tenant	
Tesco PLC	7.4%
Debenhams plc	5.7
J Sainsbury plc	5.4
Her Majesty's Government	3.4
UBS AG	3.0
Kingfisher plc (B&Q)	2.6
Home Retail Group	2.6
Next plc	2.3
Arcadia Group Ltd.	2.0
Virgin Active	1.9
Spirit Group	1.6
Alliance Boots GmbH	1.5
Herbert Smith	1.3
Marks and Spencer plc	1.2
DSG International plc	1.2
Royal Bank of Scotland plc	1.2
Aegis Group	1.1
Hutchison Whampoa Limited	1.1
TJX Companies, Inc. (TK Maxx)	1.1
House of Fraser	1.0
Industry	Percentage Share
General retailers	19%
Fashion and beauty	18
Banks and financial services	16
Supermarket operators	15
Professional and corporate	13
Food/leisure	9
Do it yourself	7
Government	3

Source: Based on data from British Land PLC, Half Year Results Presentation (September 2014).

EQUITY REITS: ASSETS

Most of an equity REIT's assets are tied to direct real estate. But within direct investments, a REIT can specialise in certain real estate subsegments.

These subsegments can include office buildings, shopping centres, residential properties, industrial properties, hotels, and so on, which are income-producing assets. Therefore, a majority of equity REITs hold a portfolio of properties that generate income, mainly from leasing.

EQUITY REITS: LIABILITIES

Equity REITs are capital-intensive firms and, relative to other equity classes, tend to hold relatively small cash positions, which is partially attributed to a legal requirement to distribute significant net income as dividends. REITs often go to the external markets to raise capital to take advantage of investment opportunities. Therefore, the financial health of equity REITs depends on their ability to access the debt market when they need it.

In broad terms, REIT borrowings can be split between secured debt and unsecured debt:

- *Secured debt.* Secured debt is tied to real estate that is considered collateral for the debt. Lenders place a lien on the property, giving them the right to take the asset if the REIT falls behind on payments.

  Secured debts can be grouped together to create a securitised vehicle, thus providing flexibility to the REIT to buy and sell property without constantly charging and discharging the collateral. However, this facility comes with certain covenant requirements and cross-collateralisation across assets. An example of such vehicle at Land Securities is shown in **Figure 4**.

- *Unsecured debt.* With unsecured debts, lenders do not have rights to any collateral for the debt. If a REIT falls behind on interest payments, lenders do not have the right to take any assets. But nonpayment can create many other problems that may threaten the existence of a REIT in its predelinquent form.

REITs often have rolling bank overdraft facilities that they use to buy any investment opportunities that may arise and subsequently refinance it by placing an unsecured private placement or issuing a secured bond against the real estate.

Figure 4. Land Securities' Security Group Structure

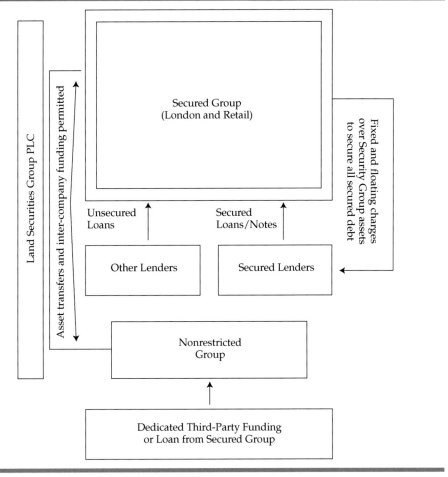

Notes: Secured Group includes Land Securities' Retail and London assets. Nonrestricted group includes joint venture interests, assets with dedicated third-party funding, and strategic land holdings.

Source: Based on data from Land Securities.

MORTGAGE REITS: REVENUE

Mortgage REITs do not buy commercial or residential real estate. Rather, they invest in real estate debt. They borrow money using short-term debt and use the funds to buy longer-term mortgages and mortgage-backed securities, earning the spread between the rates.

The primary revenue of mortgage REITs is interest income that is earned on mortgages and mortgage-backed paper during the reporting period. In broad terms, a mortgage REIT's model is similar to that of a bank. However, the revenue generated from a bank's assets consists of all forms of personal and commercial loans, mortgages, and securities, whereas a mortgage REIT only earns income from commercial or residential mortgages or MBS.

Mortgage REITs carry their investments at fair value, recognising net gains or losses on disposals and recording unrealised movements in investment values. It is common for mortgage REITs to hedge their interest rate exposure by entering into a number of interest rate swap agreements. According to generally accepted accounting practices, these swaps are marked to market and their movement in values is recognised on the income statement.

MORTGAGE REITS: EXPENSES

Mortgage REITs leverage their balance sheets to buy mortgage-backed securities, so the bulk of their expenses are to service the debt and cost of interest rate hedges. Analysts should focus on a mortgage REIT's repurchase agreements and hedges, maturity profile, and duration impact on the profit and loss account (see **Table 9**).

MORTGAGE REITS: ASSETS

Most of a mortgage REIT's investments are tied to MBS. As previously described, an MBS is a type of asset-backed security secured by a mortgage or, more commonly, a pool of mortgages. The mortgages are sold to a group of individuals (a government agency or investment bank) that "securitises", or packages, the loans together into a security that can be sold to investors.

Based on their underlying securities, MBS can be classified as either residential (RMBS) or commercial (CMBS). RMBS are a type of MBS that typically represent cash yields paid to investors and are supported by cash payments received from homeowners who pay interest and principal according to terms agreed to with their lenders. In the United States, depending on whether it is an agency MBS or a non-agency MBS, it may be issued by structures set up by government-sponsored enterprises (GSEs)—such as Fannie Mae or Freddie Mac, often referred to as US GSEs—or they can be "private label", which are issued by structures set up by investment banks. The structure of the MBS may be known as "pass-through", in which the interest and principal payments from the borrower or homebuyer pass through it to the MBS holder, or it may be more complex and made up of a pool of other MBS.

Table 9. Quarter-over-Quarter Interest Rate and MBS Spread Sensitivity of Annaly Capital Management Inc.

Interest Rate Change (bps)	As of 30 September 2014		As of 30 June 2014	
	Estimated Percentage Change in Portfolio Value[1]	Estimated Change as Percentage of NAV[1,2]	Estimated Percentage Change in Portfolio Value[1]	Estimated Change as Percentage of NAV[1,2]
Interest rate sensitivity				
−75	0.8%	5.2%	0.7%	4.5%
−50	0.7	4.5	0.6	3.9
−25	0.4	2.8	0.4	2.6
25	−0.5	−3.6	−0.5	−3.5
50	−1.2	−7.8	−1.2	−7.5
75	−1.8	−12.3	−1.8	−11.9
	Estimated Percentage Change in Portfolio Market Value	Estimated Change as Percentage of NAV[1,2]	Estimated Percentage Change in Portfolio Market Value	Estimated Change as Percentage of NAV[1,2]
MBS spread sensitivity				
−25	1.3%	8.9%	1.4%	8.8%
−15	0.8	5.3	0.8	5.3
−5	0.3	1.8	0.3	1.7
5	−0.3	−1.8	−0.3	−1.7
15	−0.8	−5.2	−0.8	−5.2
25	−1.3	−8.7	−1.3	−8.6

[1]Scenarios include investment securities and derivative instruments.
[2]NAV represents book value of common equity.
Source: Based on information from Annaly Capital Management as of September 2014.

Commercial mortgage REITs provide financing for commercial real estate. They may invest in commercial mortgages, as well as both rated and unrated CMBS, mezzanine loans, subordinated securities, or construction loans, and participate in loan securitisations.

MORTGAGE REITS: LIABILITIES

Liabilities of mortgage REITs consist of hedges and repurchase agreements. Accordingly, they are sensitive to interest rate changes. Declining short-term interest rates are positive for mortgage REITs, and inversely, a rising interest rate environment is negative. This sensitivity works opposite from equity REITs; lower interest rates are usually attributable to slower economic growth or a soft property rental cycle growth and thus a weak direct real estate market.

Mortgage REITs usually publish their sensitivity to interest rates, and it is important for an analyst to determine how the expectation of higher interest rates could affect profitability.

FORECASTING AND VALUATION

REITs are collections of individual properties. Although REITs have management teams, overhead, and other business segments, most of a REIT's value comes from the sum of its property portfolio. Therefore, it is important to understand how the property appraisal and price discovery process works and how it is relevant for the forecasting and valuation of REITs.

PROPERTY APPRAISALS, PRICE DISCOVERY, AND THE CONCEPT OF SMOOTHING

Real estate valuation methodology has traditionally been classified under five methods.

1. *Comparative method (comps).* Used for most types of property where there is good evidence of previous sales.

2. *Investment method.* Used for most commercial property that is producing cash flows and has a good visibility of its future cash flow through a contractual leasing agreement. If the current ERV and the passing income are known, as well as the market-determined equivalent yield, then the property value can be determined by a simple model, which is net rent divided by net initial yield adjusted for incentives and vacancy. Note that this method is really a comparison method because the main variables are determined in the market. In standard US practice, net operating income is used—that is, gross potential income less vacancy and collection loss less operating expenses (but excluding debt service, income taxes, and/or depreciation charges).

3. *Residual method.* Used for development properties or for properties that have the potential for refurbishment. Land with planning permission for development is also appraised based on the residual method.

4. *Profit method.* Used for trading properties where evidence of rates is limited, such as hotels, restaurants, and housing for the elderly. A three-year average of operating income (derived from the profit and loss or income statement) is capitalised using an appropriate yield. Because the variables used are inherent to the property and are not market derived, the resulting value will

be value-in-use or investment value, not market value, unless appropriate adjustments are made.

5. *Cost method.* Used for land and buildings of special character for which profit figures cannot be obtained or land and buildings for which there is no market because of their public service or heritage characteristics. Both the residual method and the cost method are usually grouped together in the United States under the cost method.

As noted, real estate is characterised by two variables that influence appraised value: the illiquidity of real estate transactions and the unique nature of individual property. These characteristics result in a behavioural bias known as "anchoring", in which the appraiser makes estimates by starting from an initial value that is adjusted to result in the final value. But the adjustments are typically insufficient, which results in the appraised value being biased towards the initial value. This concept is known as appraisal smoothing. Smoothing to a certain degree exists in the equity and debt markets, but because transaction evidence feedback is continuous, the values quickly absorb external factors. **Figure 5** and **Figure 6** detail the price discovery process in both the capital markets and the direct real estate market.

Figure 5. Price Discovery in Capital Markets

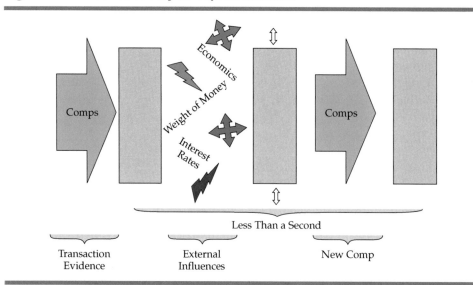

Source: Based on data from Cordea Savills.

Figure 6. Price Discovery in Direct Real Estate Markets

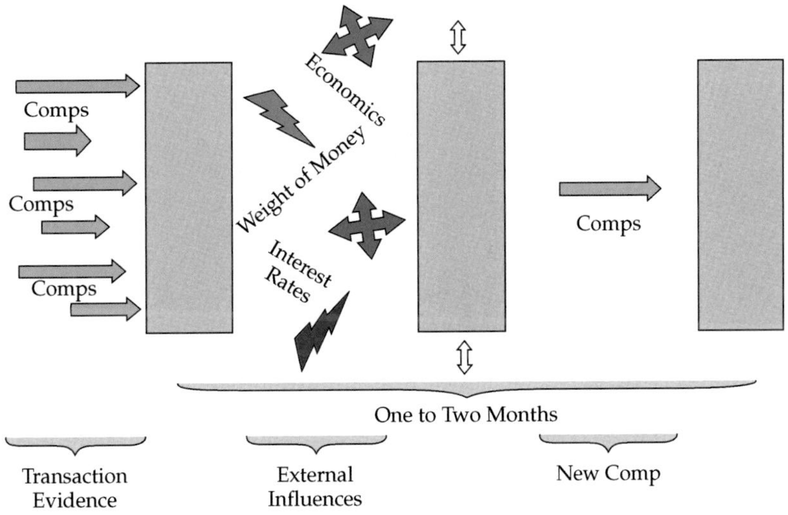
Comps
Comps
Comps
Economics
Weight of Money
Interest Rates
Comps
One to Two Months
Transaction Evidence
External Influences
New Comp

Source: Based on data from Cordea Savills.

FORECASTING—EQUITY REITS

A REIT's business model is simple: to buy real estate, collect rents, and distribute the majority of net income. Although a REIT has corporate-level expenses—such as administration, interest, and depreciation—that are not reflected in the financials of individual properties, most of its revenue and net direct expenses (specific to real estate) flow directly from its properties.

REITs grow their business by raising rents on their existing properties, acquiring new properties, developing and renovating properties, and disposing of properties.

Analysts should determine the rental income growth rate based on company guidance, investor presentations, and sector-specific industry research. **Table 10** provides an example from British Land. The rate of growth guidance should be tested against the market trend because higher sector-specific market vacancy rates and weak net absorption rates result in declining rents. Conversely, lower vacancy rates and high net absorption rates usually result in strong rental growth, which also encourages property developers to begin their development pipeline.

Once combined income is projected for existing assets, an analyst can then factor in potential new income by analysing the REIT's future development programme, which will become part of a REIT's income (see **Table 11**).

Table 10. Example of REIT Future Income Growth

Annualised Gross Rents	Cash Flow Basis (GBP millions)
Current passing rent	567
Expiry of rent-free periods	66
Completed development leases signed during the first half of 2014 included in expiry of rent-free periods	13
Fixed, minimum uplifts	12
Agreement for lease	5
2010 noncompleted developments pre-lease	19
Recently committed developments pre-lease	3
Total contracted	672
Developments—2010 completed developments to lease	14
Developments—recently committed	9
Developments—near term to lease	42
Investments—RPI and rent review uplifts	12
Investments—leasing of expiries and vacancies	16
Potential rent in five years	765
Increase	35%

Note: RPI is real property inventory.
Source: Based on data from British Land PLC, Half Year Results Presentation (September 2014).

Similarly, a combined income forecast is used to forecast portfolio value by applying the expected cap rate or net initial yields. But to refine portfolio values, individual properties can be segmented together and sector cap rate/net initial yields are used.

To better understand this approach, consider how commercial real estate is typically valued using capitalisation rates or net initial yields in the industry term. The easiest way to think about a cap rate is the return generated by a property, after operating expenses (before operating expenses for net initial yields). For example, if you buy a shop for GBP100,000 that takes in GBP6,000 per year and costs GBP3,000 per year to operate (utilities, management fees, taxes, insurance, maintenance, etc.), the net operating income would be GBP3,000, or a 3% cap rate [(6,000–3,000)/100,000] or 5.7% net initial yield (6,000/100,000/1.054); 5.4% is property acquisition cost, which includes 4% stamp duty, 1% agent's commission, and 0.4% for legal fees and other reports.

Table 11. Development Programme Analysis

As of 30 September 2014	Sector	British Land Share (%)	Sq. Ft. (thousands)	PC Calendar Year	Current Value (GBP millions)	Cost to Complete (GBP millions)[1,2]	ERV (GBP millions)[3]	Pre-Lease (GBP millions)[4]	Residential End Value (GBP millions)[5]
10–30 Brock St., Regents Place	Mixed use	100	503	Completed	423	1	20.6	20.5	118
10 Portman Square	Offices	100	134	Completed	205	3	9.9	9.4	—
Marble Arch House	Mixed use	100	87	Completed	82	3	4.6	1.7	19
39 Victoria St.	Offices	100	97	Completed	116	—	6.0	6.0	—
199 Bishopsgate	Offices	50	144	Completed	63	1	3.5	2.0	—
Whiteley Shopping, Fareham	Retail	50	321	Completed	62	—	3.1	3.0	—
Bedford St.	Residential	100	24	Completed	10	1	—	—	28
Glasgow Fort (leisure)	Retail	62	46	Completed	12	—	0.7	0.7	—
The Leadenhall Bldg.	Offices	50	601	Completed	318	19	19.1	9.8	—
5 Broadgate	Offices	50	710	2015	327	34	19.2	19.2	=
Total 2010 programme			2,667		1,618	62	86.7	72.3	165

Note: Data include the group's share of properties in joint ventures and funds (except area that is shown at 100%). PC is practical completion.

[1]From 1 October 2014 to PC.
[2]Cost to complete excludes notional interest because interest is capitalised individually on each development at our capitalisation rate.
[3]Estimated headline rental value net of rent payable under head leases (excluding tenant incentives).
[4]Excludes deals under offer.
[5]Residential development of which GBP160 million was completed or exchanged.
Source: Based on data from British Land PLC, Half Year Results Presentation (September 2014).

Care should be taken when forecasting development programme values because property appraisers are reluctant to reflect the true market value of an asset until the development is complete. Moreover, an additional provision should be made for potential contingent costs associated with property development. Cap rates or property yields tend to vary for a vacant property as opposed to an occupied property. Most of the time, REITs pre-lease their developments. However, in a rising market, a REIT may do a speculative development that does not lease until after completion. This approach can potentially result in a higher rent because occupiers prefer to pay more for a finished product.

Because REITs are constantly selling property, property sales are crucial to forecast in valuation/forecast models. For disposals, a model can assume a certain amount of asset sale net proceeds (based on historical averages or company guidance) and then a gain or loss on the sale of those assets (based on historical averages).

Liabilities are fairly straightforward to forecast. But focus should be on liabilities maturing over the next two years because management may possibly be in active negotiations to roll over the debt.

FORECASTING–MORTGAGE REITS

Mortgage REITs hold MBS as investments on their balance sheets and fund these investments with equity and debt capital. The business model of mortgage REITs is to earn a profit from the spread between interest income on their mortgage assets and the debt funding cost while managing mark-to-market movements and credit risk. Therefore, to forecast income of a mortgage REIT is to forecast interest income on the investments held. These investments are influenced by the interest yield curve, which, in turn, is influenced by interest rate expectations (see **Figure 7**).

Mortgage REITs will often hedge interest rate changes with interest rate options, swaps, swaptions, or other structured contracts to protect the REIT against changes in the interest rate curve. See **Table 12** for an example of this type of hedging.

A good understanding of the effect on a REIT's investment income from a change in the interest rate curve, investment, hedges, and the debt maturity profile is essential for an analyst to project income that a REIT will receive in the future. But care should be taken to use coupons to project income rather than mark-to-market yields.

Mortgage REITs rely on a variety of funding sources, including common and preferred equity, repurchase agreements, structured financing, convertible and long-term debt, and other credit facilities.

REITs usually borrow short term and buy investments with longer maturities. This approach creates an inherent business risk in a mortgage REIT's model that will require it to actively manage the effects of changes in short- and long-term interest rates. A mortgage REIT typically manages and mitigates risk associated with

Figure 7. Evolution of Treasury Yield Curve and Fed Policy Forecast

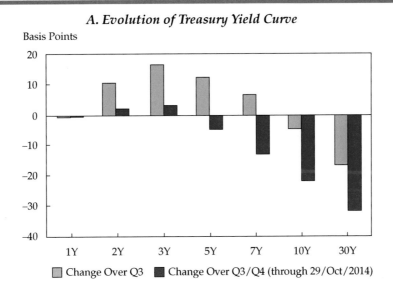

A. Evolution of Treasury Yield Curve

☐ Change Over Q3   ■ Change Over Q3/Q4 (through 29/Oct/2014)

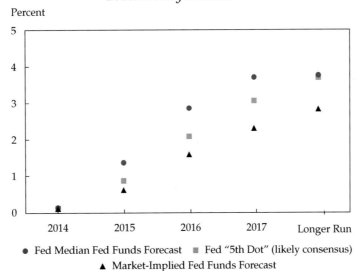

B. Fed Policy Forecast

● Fed Median Fed Funds Forecast   ■ Fed "5th Dot" (likely consensus)
▲ Market-Implied Fed Funds Forecast

Source: Based on data from Annaly Capital Management.

its short-term borrowings through conventional, widely used hedging strategies, including interest rate swaps, swaptions, interest rate collars, caps or floors, and other financial futures contracts.

Table 12. Hedging and Liabilities of Annaly Capital Management

Maturity	Current Notional[1] (USD thousands)	Weighted-Average Pay Rate[2,3]	Weighted-Average Receive Rate[2]	Weighted-Average Years to Maturity[2]
Interest rate swaps				
0 to <3 years	2,202,522	1.47%	0.16%	2.84
≥3 to <6 years	11,013,000	2.06	0.22	5.34
≥6 to <10 years	13,204,000	2.65	0.22	8.71
Greater than 10 years	5,051,800	3.58	0.19	19.78
Total/weighted average	31,471,322	2.48%	0.21%	8.61

	Current Underlying Notional (USD thousands)	Weighted-Average Underlying Pay Rate	Weighted-Average Underlying Receive Rate	Weighted-Average Underlying Years to Maturity	Weighted-Average Months to Expiration
Interest rate swaptions					
Type					
Long	1,900,000	3.13%	Three-month LIBOR	10.02	4.82
Short	—	—	—	—	—

	Principal Balance (USD thousands)	Weighted-Average Rate
Repurchase agreements		
Maturity		
Within 30 days	20,641,847	0.28%
50 to 59 days	14,241,967	0.37
60 to 89 days	2,871,206	0.38
90 to 119 days	10,548,578	0.37
Over 120 days[4]	21,307,124	1.14
Total/weighted average	69,610,722	0.58%

Note: Information is unaudited.
[1]Notional amount includes USD0.8 billion in forward starting-pay fixed swaps.
[2]Excludes forward starting swaps.
[3]Weighted-average fixed rate on forward starting-pay fixed swaps was 3.24%.
[4]Of the total repurchase agreements, approximately 12% have a remaining maturity over one year.
Source: Based on information from Annaly Capital Management as of September 2014.

Mortgage REITs also manage risk in other ways, such as adjusting the average maturities on their assets as well as borrowings and selling assets during periods of interest rate volatility to raise cash or reduce borrowings.

Understanding hedging strategies and their impact on mortgage REITs' investments and liabilities requires careful analysis because changes in interest rates affect not only the net interest income but also mark-to-market values of mortgage assets, which could have a significant impact on corporate net worth. **Table 13** lists Annaly Capital Management's investment portfolio's interest yield, LTV, and maturity along with other details. Higher interest rates or steeper interest rate curves can result in mark-to-market losses. Hence, a volatile interest rate market can make forecasting of mortgage REITs' interest income a challenging task if a REIT's exposure to the interest rate curve is not fully hedged.

Although credit impairment loss for residential mortgage REITs in the United States is limited because agency securities are backed by the federal government, commercial mortgage REITs may be exposed to credit risk. The degree of credit risk for a particular security depends on the credit performance of the underlying loans, the structure of the security (that is, which classes of security are paid first and which are paid later), and the degree of overcollateralisation (in which the face amount of the mortgage loans held as collateral exceeds the face amount of the RMBS or CMBS issued). Analysts should also discuss with the management of REITs the "single monthly mortality" rate of the underlying MBS. Single monthly mortality rate is the percentage of the principal amount of mortgages that are prepaid in a given month. For REITs, prepayment of mortgages is usually undesirable because future interest is foregone. Usually, low interest rates increase the probability that some borrowers will refinance or repay their mortgages. When such a refinancing or repayment occurs, REITs must reinvest the proceeds into the prevailing interest rate environment, which may be lower or higher. Mortgage REITs seek to hedge prepayment risk using similar tools and techniques as those they use to hedge against interest rate risks.

HOW TO VALUE A REIT

To assess the investment value of REIT shares, a typical analysis involves one or more of the following criteria:

- Current FFO yields relative to other yield-oriented investments (e.g., bonds, utility stocks, and other high-income investments)

- Underlying asset values of the real estate and/or mortgages as well as other assets

- Management quality and corporate structure

Table 13. Annaly Capital Management's Investment Portfolio

	No. of Loans	Book Values[1] (USD thousands)	Percentage of Portfolio	Yield[2]	Weighted-Average LTV[2,3]	Weighted-Average Maturity (years)[2,4]
Debt investments						
Financeable debt investments	4	111,294	7%	4.91%	67%	4.54
Securitised investments	10	398,409	26	6.03	73	3.30
Balance sheet debt investments						
Senior debt investments	3	259,991	17%	10.39%	70%	0.79
Mezzanine loan investments	29	537,654	35	10.99	75	3.88
Preferred equity investments	5	247,610	16	11.27	92	5.83
Balance sheet debt investment subtotal	37	1,045,255	67%	10.91%	78%	3.58
Total debt investments	51	1,554,958	100%	9.23%	76%	3.57

	No. of Properties	Book Value (USD thousands)	Percentage of Portfolio	Yield[5]		
Equity investments						
Real estate held for investment[6]	5	73,827	100%	8.33%		
Total equity investments	5	73,827	100%	8.33%		

Note: Information is unaudited.
[1]Book values include net origination fees.
[2]Total weighted based on book value.
[3]Based on most recent third-party appraisal, which may be prior to loan origination/purchase date, and on an "as is" basis at the time of underwriting.
[4]Maturity dates assume all of the borrowers' extension options are exercised.
[5]Total weighted based on net equity investment value.
[6]Yield on existing investments with 12 or more months of Annaly operating history is based on GAAP net income, excluding depreciation and amortisation expense, utilising trailing 12-month operating results and net economic equity at 30 September 2014. Weighted-average Year 1 yield on current year property acquisitions is 7.5% (net of acquisition fees and closing expenses). Stabilised leveraged yield on current year property acquisitions is estimated to be approximately 13.3%.
Source: Based on information from Annaly Capital Management as of September 2014.

It is difficult to value a REIT based on traditional metrics, such as earnings per share ratio, growth, the price-to-earnings multiple, and so on. The price of a REIT is based primarily on its anticipated income stream and an assessment of its management structure, the underlying asset values, and the potential for capital appreciation.

Assuming an investment in a REIT yields x% compared with alternative investments yielding y%, the investor assesses whether the spread provides adequate compensation for the incremental risk associated with a REIT investment.

Recently, there have been conflicting views among investors, analysts, and management about how REITs should report profitability and what is the most effective measure of a REIT's performance. This debate is ongoing because many believe that current reporting practices of REITs do not allow for comparability with other companies in the market.

A REIT's value is derived from its ability to deliver consistent cash distributions, as well as appreciation of the underlying assets. In periods of low expected capital appreciation and low interest rates, the valuation emphasis will be on yield. Yield is typically calculated by dividing the following year's target distributions per unit by the current market price per unit.

Taxable investors will be interested in the post-tax yield, whereas nontaxable investors will concentrate on pre-tax yield. Even if the pre-tax income of the trust remains constant, the post-tax yield will change over time as the tax shelter in the REIT changes.

FFO is more commonly used as a metric to value REITs and their growth potential, but the measure contains a weakness: it does not deduct for capital expenditures required to maintain the existing portfolio of properties. Investment holdings in real estate must be maintained (for example, apartments must be painted), so FFO is not quite the true residual cash flow remaining after all expenses and expenditures.

As a result, the "adjusted funds from operations" measure is recommended. Although FFO is commonly used, analysts tend to focus on AFFO for two reasons. First, it is a more precise measure of residual cash flow available to shareholders and thus a better "base number" for estimating value (for example, applying a multiple or discounting a future stream of AFFO). Second, because it is true residual cash flow, it is a better predictor of the REIT's future capacity to pay dividends.

AFFO does not have a uniform definition; however, the most important adjustment made to calculate AFFO is subtracting capital expenditures, as mentioned earlier.

Once analysts have the FFO and the AFFO, they can try to estimate the value of the REIT. The key assumption here is the expected growth in FFO or AFFO, which involves taking a careful look at the underlying prospects of the REIT and its sector. The specifics of evaluating a REIT's growth prospects should include

- prospects for rent increases and

- prospects to improve/maintain occupancy rates.

REITs often undertake redevelopment of properties to attract a higher-quality tenant. Often a virtuous cycle ensues, by which better tenants lead to higher occupancy rates (fewer evictions) and higher rents.

Many REITs grow FFO through acquisitions. However, because a REIT must distribute most of its profits, it does not have a lot of excess capital to deploy. Nevertheless, REITs often actively recycle their capital, selling underperforming assets to finance the acquisition of new and presumably undervalued properties.

The total return on a REIT investment comes from two sources: (1) dividends paid and (2) price appreciation. Therefore, its growth can be broken down into two components:

- Growth in FFO/AFFO

- Expansion in the price-to-FFO or price-to-AFFO multiple

AFFO yield, in addition to being one measure of valuation, is often used as a proxy for a company's nominal cost of capital. It is calculated by dividing a company's per-share AFFO estimate by its stock price. If a company with an AFFO yield of 6.5% buys a property at a going-in-stabilised return of 7.5%, it has acquired the property at a 100 bp (or 1 percentage point) positive spread to its nominal cost of capital.

A primary drawback of AFFO is that it does not incorporate property appreciation or depreciation. The result is that in years when properties are falling in value, stripping out depreciation can artificially inflate REIT shares and mask underlying problems. In other words, slight drops in FFO from higher vacancies or lower rents may hide higher risks posed to investors by falling property values.

Therefore, it is important to look at the total value of assets. This value is particularly important at times when interest rates are changing because higher (or lower) implied inflation may result in higher (or lower) rents and thus capital appreciation (decline) of the underlying real estate assets.

During such times, investors who seek a means by which to measure the future capital appreciation potential will likely begin considering the discount or premium to NAV in their valuation.

NAV analysis is central to many investors' thinking when it comes to investing in REITs and non-REIT real estate operating companies. But NAV is only one of a number of valuation metrics. Like any metric, it has its pros and cons. For example, the calculation of NAV is admittedly more art than science. It is also important to keep in mind that NAV is a leveraged number. The more highly leveraged a company is, for instance, the more pronounced the impact changes in property yields will have on the resulting NAV.

Similarly, as highlighted, property valuers assign low values to empty space. Therefore, assigning a value to the unleased space within many companies' portfolios, especially those REITs whose occupancy rates are substantially depressed and well below a normalised occupancy figure, could have a material impact on its valuation.

This method, however, is favoured in a majority of European countries because it allows an analyst to break down values by an individual property. Ultimately, it is the underlying property values that are combined together to form the portfolio value of a REIT.

In a rising market, the value of a REIT can trade above its NAV per share or below if direct markets are softening. But over the long run (greater than 20 years), the average discount/premium to NAV for the overall market has been roughly 0%.

There are a number of factors to keep in mind when using NAVs in the construction of a valuation matrix. For instance, because cap rates are central to the calculation of NAV, during periods when few transactions are taking place, the calculation of NAV can be problematic. At the same time, during periods when companies are rapidly expanding or contracting their portfolios, getting a fix on NAV is more difficult, if not impossible.

Furthermore, analysts trying to understand true NAV may need to adjust the portfolio value of a REIT by reflecting the fair value of debt and derivatives and to include deferred taxation on revaluations. This metric is also known as "triple nets".

WHAT TO LOOK FOR IN A REIT

Although the following list is not exhaustive, it lists the main characteristics that are widely accepted and rewarded by the market.

- REITs with an experienced manager that has a proven track record for the specific type of REIT are rewarded. This characteristic is not meant to discourage newly launched REITs, but it is important that the management has relevant experience in the sector.

- Diversification in REITs primarily occurs in two ways: property type and geography. But focus on a specific sector often results in economies of scale and expertise. Therefore, investors should target REITs with a focused portfolio (i.e., by either property type or location).

- REITs need to have strong net operating income, cash flow, and sustainable income growth.

- Low debt is attractive. REITs that have debt of more than 60% of their market capitalisation have been penalised by the market in the past.

- Management holding a significant investment in the REIT (10%–20%) is expected to align management's behaviour with investors' goals.

- REITs need sufficient size to capture the brokerage community's interest, to ensure adequate liquidity, and to attract institutional investors. The REIT must have also achieved economies of scale with respect to its fixed overhead costs (i.e., the REIT's initial asset size should be in excess of USD250 million with an ability to quickly grow its asset base to more than USD500 million).

■ Secondary offerings are often dilutive and thus potentially negative for equityholders. Therefore, REITs that have been active with secondary offerings should be closely scrutinized. **Figure 8** shows secondary equity offerings by US REITs.

■ A REIT should have distributions in the range of 80%–95% of its net income. This level of distributions will allow the REIT to use its retained operating funds to grow its asset size without going to the market for potentially dilutive (at least in the short term) capital issuance.

The following are secondary factors to consider in a REIT:

■ Tenant lease maturity and exposure profile (a REIT may have significant exposure to one tenant, and the failure of that tenant could result in a significant impact on REIT viability)

■ Obligations to distribute income as per local REIT regulations and withholding tax on dividend payments

■ Level of disclosure in reporting to unitholders

Figure 8. Secondary Equity Offerings by US REITs

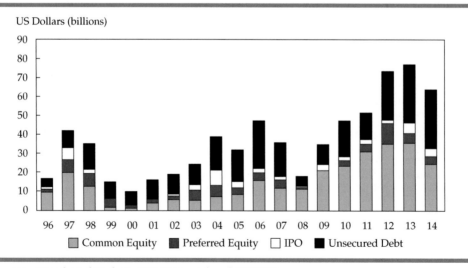

Sources: Based on data from SNL Financial and NAREIT.

- Investment criteria for new properties
- Environmental risks and controls
- Nonconflict and noncompetition provisions for the manager
- Governance issues

US AND EUROPEAN REITS

Table 14 presents a comparative analysis of US REITs by sector. **Table 15** presents European REITs.

Table 14. US REIT Comparative Analysis, as of 13 March 2015

Sector/Company (Ticker)	Price (USD)	Total Equity Market Cap (USD millions)	Total Debt (USD millions)	Total Market Value (USD millions)	Debt to Total Market Value	Net Debt to Recurring EBITDA	EV/ Recurring EBITDA	2013 FFO per Share	2013 CAD per Share	Indicated Dividend	Dividend Yield	Barclays NAV	Price/ Barclays NAV
Apartments													
Associated Estates Realty Corporation (AEC)	23.96	1,381.3	749.1	2,130.4	35.16%	7.1×	20.2×	1.26	1.11	0.84	3.51%	20.01	119.7%
Apartment Investment and Management Company (AIV)	38.50	6,117.3	4,163.4	10,280.6	40.50	7.4	18.4	2.04	1.53	1.12	2.91	36.53	105.4
AvalonBay Communities, Inc. (AVB)	171.22	22,611.0	6,588.5	29,199.4	22.56	5.4	25.6	4.96	4.83	5.00	2.92	155.20	110.3
Camden Property Trust (CPT)	75.63	6,695.2	2,743.5	9,438.8	29.07	5.1	18.4	4.11	3.32	2.80	3.70	85.30	88.7
Equity Residential (EQR)	77.13	29,139.9	10,844.9	39,984.8	27.12	6.1	22.7	2.36	2.02	2.21	2.87	75.01	102.8
Essex Property Trust, Inc. (ESS)	228.77	15,143.6	5,109.8	20,253.4	25.23	6.4	25.6	7.59	6.85	5.76	2.52	199.54	114.6
Home Properties, Inc. (HME)	66.42	4,504.5	2,456.2	6,960.7	35.29	5.9	16.7	4.37	3.84	3.04	4.58	71.17	93.3
Mid-America Apartment (MAA)	73.94	5,875.2	3,524.5	9,399.7	37.50	6.2	16.6	4.29	3.82	3.08	4.17	72.18	102.4

(continued)

Table 14. US REIT Comparative Analysis, as of 13 March 2015 (continued)

Sector/ Company (Ticker)	Price (USD)	Total Equity Market Cap (USD millions)	Total Debt (USD millions)	Total Market Value (USD millions)	Debt to Total Market Value	Net Debt to Recurring EBITDA	EV/ Recurring EBITDA	2013 FFO per Share	2013 CAD per Share	Indicated Dividend	Dividend Yield	Barclays NAV	Price/ Barclays NAV
Apartments (continued)													
Post Properties, Inc. (PPS)	55.38	3,068.8	892.5	3,961.2	22.53%	3.8×	19.5×	3.01	2.47	1.60	2.89%	58.33	94.9%
UDR, Inc. (UDR)	32.75	8,644.4	3,583.1	12,227.5	29.30	7.1	24.3	1.44	1.23	1.11	3.39	31.32	104.6
Apartment total/weighted average		103,181.0	40,655.4	143,836.5	28.27%	6.1×	22.6×				3.09%		105.1%
Commercial debt													
Colony Financial (CLNY)	25.39	3,121.9	2,748.2	5,870.0	46.82%	NM	NM	1.23	NA	1.48	5.83%	NA	NA
NorthStar Realty Finance (NRF)	18.19	6,426.8	9,986.4	16,413.2	60.84	NM	NM	0.14	NA	1.60	8.80	NA	NA
Starwood Property Trust (STWD)	23.71	5,300.1	4,685.3	9,985.3	46.92	NM	NM	2.02	NA	1.92	8.10	NA	NA
Commercial debt/equity total/weighted average		14,848.7	17,419.8	32,268.5	53.98%	NA	NA				7.92%		NA
Commercial mortgage													
Arbor Realty Trust (ABR)	6.98	445.1	1,260.0	1,705.1	73.90%	NM	NM	0.37	NA	0.52	7.45%	NA	NA

(continued)

Table 14. US REIT Comparative Analysis, as of 13 March 2015 (continued)

Sector/Company (Ticker)	Price (USD)	Total Equity Market Cap (USD millions)	Total Debt (USD millions)	Total Market Value (USD millions)	Debt to Total Market Value	Net Debt to Recurring EBITDA	EV/Recurring EBITDA	2013 FFO per Share	2013 CAD per Share	Indicated Dividend	Dividend Yield	Barclays NAV	Price/Barclays NAV
Commercial mortgage (continued)													
Apollo Commercial Real Estate Finance (ARI)	16.84	876.1	868.7	1,744.7	49.79%	NM	NM	1.27	1.45	1.76	10.45%	16.35	103.0%
Blackstone Mortgage Trust (BXMT)	28.29	1,648.5	3,026.6	4,675.1	64.74	NM	NM	0.91	NA	2.08	7.35	NA	NA
Newcastle Investment Corp (NCT)	4.66	371.1	1,315.2	1,686.3	77.99	NM	NM	4.17	2.73	0.48	10.30	5.93	78.5
RAIT Financial Trust (RAS)	7.27	817.4	2,615.7	3,433.1	76.19	NM	NM	-2.51	NA	0.72	9.90	NA	NA
iStar Financial (STAR)	12.80	1,835.4	4,022.7	5,858.1	68.67	NM	NM	-0.99	NA	0.00	0.00	NA	NA
Commercial mortgage total/weighted average		5,993.6	13,108.9	19,102.5	68.62%	NA	NA				6.09%		95.7%
Diversified													
Cousins Properties Inc. (CUZ)	10.34	2,238.7	792.3	3,031.1	26.14%	3.5×	13.4×	0.51	NA	0.32	3.09%	NA	NA
Winthrop Realty Trust (FUR)	16.05	584.6	475.4	1,060.0	44.85	17.4	40.4	1.34	1.20	0.00	0.00	17.00	94.4%
Investors Real Estate Trust (IRET)	7.11	1,095.3	1,053.7	2,148.9	49.03	6.2	13.1	NA	NA	0.52	7.31	NA	NA

(continued)

Table 14. US REIT Comparative Analysis, as of 13 March 2015 (continued)

Sector/Company (Ticker)	Price (USD)	Total Equity Market Cap (USD millions)	Total Debt (USD millions)	Total Market Value (USD millions)	Debt to Total Market Value	Net Debt to Recurring EBITDA	EV/ Recurring EBITDA	2013 FFO per Share	2013 CAD per Share	Indicated Dividend	Dividend Yield	Barclays NAV	Price/ Barclays NAV
Diversified (continued)													
Washington Real Estate Investment Trust (WRE)	26.97	1,829.1	1,215.7	3,044.8	39.93%	6.8×	17.1×	1.75	NA	1.20	4.45%	NA	NA
Diversified total/weighted average		5,747.7	3,537.1	9,284.8	38.10%	6.5×	17.2×				4.01%		94.4%
Health care													
Health Care REIT (HCN)	75.30	25,764.1	10,828.0	36,592.2	29.59%	6.1×	21.3×	3.78	NA	3.30	4.38%	NA	NA
Healthcare Property Investors (HCP)	40.33	18,786.8	9,759.8	28,546.5	34.19	5.1	15.2	2.97	NA	2.26	5.60	NA	NA
Healthcare Realty Trust, Inc. (HR)	26.73	2,641.7	1,403.7	4,045.4	34.70	6.3	18.1	1.06	NA	1.20	4.49	NA	NA
LTC Properties Inc. (LTC)	43.43	1,579.4	281.6	1,861.0	15.13	2.3	16.7	2.34	NA	2.04	4.70	NA	NA
Medical Properties Trust Inc. (MPW)	14.36	2,484.4	2,201.7	4,686.1	46.98	9.4	20.7	0.96	NA	0.88	6.13	NA	NA
National Health Investors Inc. (NHI)	68.52	2,568.5	862.7	3,431.3	25.14	4.9	19.7	3.48	NA	3.40	4.96	NA	NA

(continued)

Table 14. US REIT Comparative Analysis, as of 13 March 2015 (continued)

Sector/Company (Ticker)	Price (USD)	Total Equity Market Cap (USD millions)	Total Debt (USD millions)	Total Market Value (USD millions)	Debt to Total Market Value	Net Debt to Recurring EBITDA	EV/Recurring EBITDA	2013 FFO per Share	2013 CAD per Share	Indicated Dividend	Dividend Yield	Barclays NAV	Price/Barclays NAV
Health care (continued)													
Omega Healthcare Investors (OHI)	39.50	5,040.4	2,378.5	7,418.9	32.06%	4.9×	15.4×	2.52	NA	2.16	5.47%	NA	NA
Senior Housing Properties Trust (SNH)	21.59	4,402.4	2,800.7	7,203.1	38.88	5.5	14.3	1.68	NA	1.56	7.23	NA	NA
Universal Health Realty Income Trust (UHT)	52.45	697.6	213.2	910.8	23.40	4.6	19.8	NA	NA	2.54	4.84	NA	NA
Ventas, Inc (VTR)	70.37	21,159.6	10,931.6	32,091.2	34.06	6.2	18.1	4.13	NA	3.16	4.49	NA	NA
Health care total/weighted average		85,125.0	41,661.4	126,786.5	32.86%	5.8×	18.2×				4.97%		NA
Hotels													
Ashford Hospitality Trust (AHT)	9.95	1,481.2	1,954.1	3,435.3	56.88%	9.7×	18.0×	1.16	NA	0.48	4.82%	NA	NA
Strategic Hotels & Resorts Inc. (BEE)	12.31	3,301.9	1,796.2	5,098.1	35.23	4.9	16.8	0.42	NA	0.00	0.00	NA	NA
DiamondRock Hospitality Company (DRH)	14.45	2,889.5	1,038.3	3,927.8	26.44	3.8	16.2	0.73	NA	0.50	3.46	NA	NA

(continued)

Table 14.   US REIT Comparative Analysis, as of 13 March 2015 (continued)

Sector/ Company (Ticker)	Price (USD)	Total Equity Market Cap (USD millions)	Total Debt (USD millions)	Total Market Value (USD millions)	Debt to Total Market Value	Net Debt to Recurring EBITDA	EV/ Recurring EBITDA	2013 FFO per Share	2013 CAD per Share	Indicated Dividend	Dividend Yield	Barclays NAV	Price/ Barclays NAV
Hotels (continued)													
FelCor Lodging Trust Inc. (FCH)	10.91	1,844.9	1,585.9	3,430.7	46.23%	8.4×	18.5×	0.38	NA	0.16	1.47%	NA	NA
Hospitality Properties Trust (HPT)	31.58	5,014.6	2,838.6	7,853.2	36.15	4.2	11.5	2.96	NA	1.96	6.21	NA	NA
Host Hotels & Resorts (HST)	20.85	15,955.6	3,992.0	19,947.6	20.01	2.3	13.5	1.28	NA	0.80	3.84	NA	NA
Hersha Hospitality Trust (HT)	6.54	1,541.3	918.9	2,460.2	37.35	6.1	16.7	0.40	NA	0.28	4.28	NA	NA
LaSalle Hotel Properties (LHO)	39.29	4,623.3	1,072.2	5,695.4	18.82	3.0	17.7	2.28	NA	1.50	3.82	NA	NA
Pebblebrook Hotel Trust (PEB)	46.64	3,687.8	844.0	4,531.8	18.62	4.5	25.3	1.44	NA	1.24	2.66	NA	NA
Sunstone Hotel Investors (SHO)	16.40	3,473.2	1,444.9	4,918.0	29.38	4.0	15.3	0.91	NA	0.20	1.22	NA	NA
Hotels total/ weighted average		43,813.2	17,485.0	61,298.2	28.52%	3.8×	15.7×				3.43%		
Industrial													
DCT Industrial Trust Inc. (DCT)	34.15	3,149.1	1,409.0	4,558.1	30.91%	6.3×	20.5×	1.79	4.26	1.12	3.28%	30.31	112.7%

(continued)

Table 14. US REIT Comparative Analysis, as of 13 March 2015 (continued)

Sector/Company (Ticker)	Price (USD)	Total Equity Market Cap (USD millions)	Total Debt (USD millions)	Total Market Value (USD millions)	Debt to Total Market Value	Net Debt to Recurring EBITDA	EV/Recurring EBITDA	2013 FFO per Share	2013 CAD per Share	Indicated Dividend	Dividend Yield	Barclays NAV	Price/Barclays NAV
Industrial (continued)													
EastGroup Properties Inc. (EGP)	58.66	1,890.8	933.2	2,823.9	33.05%	6.2×	18.7×	3.23	2.34	2.28	3.89%	54.64	107.4%
First Industrial Realty Trust (FR)	20.73	2,383.4	1,349.8	3,733.3	36.16	6.2	17.2	0.98	0.59	0.51	2.46	20.48	101.2
Monmouth Real Estate Investment Corp. (MNR)	11.05	749.8	364.6	1,114.4	32.72	6.0	19.0	0.63	NA	0.60	5.43	NA	NA
Prologis (PLD)	42.56	21,918.0	9,380.2	31,298.2	29.97	8.2	28.3	1.67	1.81	1.44	3.38	46.86	90.8
Industrial total/weighted average		30,091.0	13,436.9	43,528.0	30.87%	7.7×	25.7×				3.38%		95.1%
Manufactured homes													
Equity LifeStyle Properties, Inc. (ELS)	54.35	5,088.1	2,212.2	7,300.3	30.30%	6.0×	20.1×	2.09	NA	1.50	2.76%	NA	NA
Sun Communities, Inc. (SUI)	67.98	3,571.9	1,832.1	5,404.0	33.90	9.6	29.1	3.15	NA	2.60	3.82	NA	NA
Manufactured homes total/weighted average		8,660.0	4,044.3	12,704.3	31.83%	7.4×	23.8×				3.20%		NA

(continued)

Table 14. US REIT Comparative Analysis, as of 13 March 2015 (continued)

Sector/Company (Ticker)	Price (USD)	Total Equity Market Cap (USD millions)	Total Debt (USD millions)	Total Market Value (USD millions)	Debt to Total Market Value	Net Debt to Recurring EBITDA	EV/ Recurring EBITDA	2013 FFO per Share	2013 CAD per Share	Indicated Dividend	Dividend Yield	Barclays NAV	Price/ Barclays NAV
Net lease													
American Realty Capital Properties, Inc. (ARCP)	10.02	10,415.8	12,157.6	22,573.3	53.86%	8.6×	16.0×	0.66	NA	0.00	0.00%	NA	NA
Gramercy Property Trust Inc. (GPT)	7.07	1,406.1	469.5	1,875.6	25.03	3.8	23.7	6.66	NA	0.20	2.83	NA	NA
Lexington Realty Trust (LXP)	9.96	2,455.8	2,095.5	4,551.3	46.04	5.4	12.4	0.88	0.58	0.68	6.83	9.52	104.7%
National Retail Properties, Inc. (NNN)	39.83	5,813.3	1,741.1	7,554.3	23.05	4.2	18.4	1.91	NA	1.68	4.22	NA	NA
Realty Income Corporation (O)	50.14	11,711.9	4,942.1	16,654.0	29.68	6.0	20.3	2.40	NA	2.27	4.54	NA	NA
STORE Capital (STOR)	21.76	2,507.0	1,284.2	3,791.2	33.87	5.9	0.0	NA	NA	1.02	4.70	NA	NA
W.P. Carey Inc. (WPC)	67.34	7,006.1	4,088.5	11,094.6	36.85	6.2	17.3	2.98	NA	3.80	5.64	NA	NA
Net lease total/weighted average		41,315.9	26,778.4	68,094.3	39.33%	6.3×	16.9×				3.62%		104.7%
Office													
Alexandria Real Estate Equities, Inc. (ARE)	97.46	7,326.9	3,678.6	11,005.5	33.42%	7.6×	23.0×	4.33	4.05	2.96	3.04%	78.40	124.3%

(continued)

Table 14. US REIT Comparative Analysis, as of 13 March 2015 (continued)

Sector/Company (Ticker)	Price (USD)	Total Equity Market Cap (USD millions)	Total Debt (USD millions)	Total Market Value (USD millions)	Debt to Total Market Value	Net Debt to Recurring EBITDA	EV/Recurring EBITDA	2013 FFO per Share	2013 CAD per Share	Indicated Dividend	Dividend Yield	Barclays NAV	Price/Barclays NAV
Office (continued)													
Brandywine Realty Trust (BDN)	15.21	2,840.8	2,451.3	5,292.1	46.32%	6.6×	15.3×	1.35	0.72	0.60	3.94%	17.00	89.5%
BioMed Realty Trust (BMR)	22.03	4,468.7	2,719.7	7,188.4	37.83	7.1	18.9	1.47	NA	1.04	4.72	NA	NA
Boston Properties Inc. (BXP)	137.34	23,687.6	10,087.0	33,774.6	29.87	5.5	21.3	4.91	3.62	2.60	1.89	136.62	100.5
Mack-Cali Realty Corp. (CLI)	18.89	1,892.0	2,088.7	3,980.7	52.47	9.0	17.2	2.38	1.61	0.60	3.18	19.65	96.1
Douglas Emmett, Inc. (DEI)	28.12	4,073.7	3,435.3	7,509.0	45.75	8.8	19.4	1.49	1.18	0.84	2.99	27.10	103.8
Equity Commonwealth (EQC)	26.00	3,754.4	2,207.7	5,962.1	37.03	4.6	14.1	2.43	NA	1.00	3.85	NA	NA
Franklin Street Properties Corp. (FSP)	12.47	1,249.3	888.0	2,137.3	41.55	6.6	16.1	1.04	NA	0.76	6.09	NA	NA
Government Properties Income Trust (GOV)	22.54	1,585.7	1,085.1	2,670.8	40.63	6.3	15.7	2.12	NA	1.72	7.63	NA	NA
Hudson Pacific Properties (HPP)	32.01	2,359.5	960.5	3,320.0	28.93	8.6	30.0	1.02	0.04	0.50	1.56	26.84	119.3

(continued)

Table 14. US REIT Comparative Analysis, as of 13 March 2015 (continued)

Sector/ Company (Ticker)	Price (USD)	Total Equity Market Cap (USD millions)	Total Debt (USD millions)	Total Market Value (USD millions)	Debt to Total Market Value	Net Debt to Recurring EBITDA	EV/ Recurring EBITDA	2013 FFO per Share	2013 CAD per Share	Indicated Dividend	Dividend Yield	Barclays NAV	Price/ Barclays NAV
Office (continued)													
Corporate Office Properties Trust (OFC)	29.23	3,037.1	1,920.1	4,957.2	38.73%	6.9×	17.7×	1.96	NA	1.10	3.76%	NA	NA
Piedmont Office Realty Trust (PDM)	17.96	2,771.7	2,277.6	5,049.2	45.11	7.2	16.0	1.47	NA	0.84	4.68	NA	NA
Paramount Group Inc. (PGRE)	19.12	5,041.0	2,894.5	7,935.5	36.48	11.1	34.0	NA	NA	0.38	1.99	NA	NA
Parkway Properties (PKY)	16.92	1,880.3	1,821.0	3,701.2	49.20	6.9	14.6	0.90	0.66	0.75	4.43	20.73	81.6%
SL Green Realty Corp. (SLG)	127.35	13,122.3	8,453.6	21,575.8	39.18	8.7	22.7	5.16	3.76	2.40	1.88	107.33	118.7
Vornado Realty Trust (VNO)	106.24	22,374.8	11,138.9	33,513.6	33.24	6.6	21.3	3.41	3.18	2.52	2.37	92.59	114.7
Office total/ weighted average		101,465.8	58,107.3	159,573.0	36.41%	7.1×	21.2×				2.72%		109.5%
Office/Industrial													
Duke Realty (DRE)	20.66	7,186.1	4,453.4	11,639.5	38.26%	7.1×	18.5×	1.07	0.89	0.68	3.29%	20.07	102.9%
First Potomac Realty Trust (FPO)	11.75	876.5	813.6	1,690.1	48.14	8.5	17.8	0.96	NA	0.60	5.11	NA	NA

(continued)

Table 14. US REIT Comparative Analysis, as of 13 March 2015 (continued)

Sector/Company (Ticker)	Price (USD)	Total Equity Market Cap (USD millions)	Total Debt (USD millions)	Total Market Value (USD millions)	Debt to Total Market Value	Net Debt to Recurring EBITDA	EV/Recurring EBITDA	2013 FFO per Share	2013 CAD per Share	Indicated Dividend	Dividend Yield	Barclays NAV	Price/Barclays NAV
Office/Industrial (continued)													
Highwoods Properties Inc. (HIW)	43.72	4,219.4	2,071.4	6,290.8	32.93%	5.7×	17.4×	2.81	NA	1.70	3.89%	NA	NA
Kilroy Realty Corp. (KRC)	73.86	6,696.8	2,469.4	9,166.2	26.94	6.7	25.1	2.63	1.49	1.40	1.90	36.76	200.9%
Liberty Property Trust (LPT)	34.91	5,310.2	3,163.4	8,473.6	37.33	5.7	15.6	2.50	NA	1.90	NA	NA	NA
PS Business Parks (PSB)	79.75	3,724.4	250.0	3,974.4	6.29	0.4	15.9	4.80	NA	2.00	2.51	NA	NA
Office/industrial total/weighted average		28,013.4	13,221.2	41,234.7	32.06%	5.7×	19.0×				2.93%		150.2%
Real estate C-corporations													
Forest City Enterprises, Inc. (FCEA)	24.89	4,952.4	4,938.2	9,890.6	49.93%	11.4×	23.7×	0.91	NA	0.00	0.00%	NA	NA
The St. Joe Company (JOE)	17.25	1,592.2	241.1	1,833.4	13.15	17.3	150.8	0.04	NA	0.00	0.00	NA	NA
Real estate C-corps total/weighted average		6,544.6	5,179.3	11,724.0	44.18%	12.9×	54.6×				0.00%		NA

(continued)

Table 14. US REIT Comparative Analysis, as of 13 March 2015 (continued)

Sector/Company (Ticker)	Price (USD)	Total Equity Market Cap (USD millions)	Total Debt (USD millions)	Total Market Value (USD millions)	Debt to Total Market Value	Net Debt to Recurring EBITDA	EV/Recurring EBITDA	2013 FFO per Share	2013 CAD per Share	Indicated Dividend	Dividend Yield	Barclays NAV	Price/Barclays NAV
Real estate services													
CBRE Group, Inc. (CBG)	34.99	11,647.0	2,424.1	14,071.1	17.23%	3.6×	3.9×	1.43	1.43	0.00	0.00%	NA	NA
Jones Lang LaSalle (JLL)	161.15	7,224.2	377.9	7,602.1	4.97	1.1	4.8	6.32	6.32	0.42	0.26	NA	NA
Real estate services total/weighted average		18,871.2	2,802.0	21,673.2	12.93%	2.6×	4.2×				0.10%		NA
Retail: regional malls													
Tanger Factory Outlet Centers (SKT)	35.29	3,549.8	1,443.2	4,993.0	28.90%	5.6×	19.4×	1.91	NA	0.96	2.72%	NA	NA
CBL & Associates Properties (CBL)	19.04	4,425.4	4,700.5	9,125.8	51.51	6.2	12.0	2.23	1.63	1.06	5.57	24.22	78.6%
General Growth Properties (GGP)	29.23	26,248.6	16,216.6	42,465.1	38.19	8.2	21.8	1.13	0.88	0.68	2.33	20.83	140.3
Macerich Co. (MAC)	92.31	15,574.6	6,292.4	21,867.0	28.78	8.0	27.9	3.53	2.80	2.60	2.82	78.78	117.2
Pennsylvania REIT (PEI)	22.20	1,768.7	1,537.9	3,306.7	46.51	6.3	13.6	1.82	1.06	0.84	3.78	28.85	76.9

(continued)

Table 14. US REIT Comparative Analysis, as of 13 March 2015 (continued)

Sector/Company (Ticker)	Price (USD)	Total Equity Market Cap (USD millions)	Total Debt (USD millions)	Total Market Value (USD millions)	Debt to Total Market Value	Net Debt to Recurring EBITDA	EV/ Recurring EBITDA	2013 FFO per Share	2013 CAD per Share	Indicated Dividend	Dividend Yield	Barclays NAV	Price/ Barclays NAV
Retail: regional malls (continued)													
Rouse Properties Inc. (RSE)	18.81	1,086.2	1,618.0	2,704.1	59.83%	10.0×	16.7×	NA	NA	0.72	3.83%	NA	NA
Simon Property Group Inc. (SPG)	183.60	66,803.2	20,853.0	87,656.2	23.79	5.0	21.7	8.85	7.69	5.60	3.05	181.00	101.4%
Taubman Centers Inc. (TCO)	77.12	7,172.7	2,025.5	9,198.2	22.02	4.4	22.3	3.60	2.62	2.26	2.93	85.60	90.1
Washington Prime Group Inc. (WPG)	16.53	3,086.8	2,348.9	5,435.6	43.21	4.9	11.7	NA	NA	0.44	2.66	NA	NA
Retail: regional malls total/weighted average		129,715.8	57,035.9	186,751.7	30.54%	6.1×	21.7×				2.95%		110.0%
Retail: shopping centre													
Acadia Realty Trust (AKR)	34.01	2,441.0	1,130.5	3,571.5	31.65%	7.0×	25.9×	1.27	0.87	0.96	2.82%	26.13	130.1%
Saul Centers (BFS)	56.36	1,355.1	857.4	2,212.4	38.75	6.2	16.1	2.61	NA	1.72	3.05	NA	NA
Brixmor Property Group (BRX)	25.17	7,657.9	6,043.0	13,700.9	44.11	7.2	16.4	1.67	0.99	0.90	3.58	22.56	111.6
Cedar Realty Trust (CDR)	7.29	746.6	665.4	1,412.0	47.12	7.5	15.9	0.50	NA	0.20	2.74	NA	NA

(continued)

Table 14. US REIT Comparative Analysis, as of 13 March 2015 (continued)

Retail: shopping centre (continued)

Sector/ Company (Ticker)	Price (USD)	Total Equity Market Cap (USD millions)	Total Debt (USD millions)	Total Market Value (USD millions)	Debt to Total Market Value	Net Debt to Recurring EBITDA	EV/ Recurring EBITDA	2013 FFO per Share	2013 CAD per Share	Indicated Dividend	Dividend Yield	Barclays NAV	Price/ Barclays NAV
DDR Corp. (DDR)	18.52	7,038.8	5,234.7	12,273.5	42.65%	7.7×	18.2×	1.10	0.89	0.69	3.73%	17.16	108.0%
Equity One, Inc. (EQY)	26.63	3,335.7	1,333.0	4,668.7	28.55	6.0	21.2	1.17	0.85	0.88	3.30	21.35	124.7
Excel Trust (EXL)	13.84	859.9	829.5	1,689.4	49.10	8.8	18.1	0.92	0.84	0.72	5.20	12.74	108.6
Federal Realty Investment Trust (FRT)	141.12	9,821.1	2,409.7	12,230.8	19.70	5.1	26.4	4.56	3.53	3.48	2.47	107.24	131.6
Inland Real Estate Corp. (IRC)	10.55	1,260.9	824.8	2,085.7	39.54	6.8	17.4	0.96	NA	0.57	5.40	NA	NA
Kimco Realty Corp. (KIM)	26.08	11,725.9	4,620.3	16,346.2	28.27	6.9	25.0	1.34	1.07	0.96	3.68	19.75	132.1
Kite Realty Group Trust (KRG)	26.85	2,384.5	1,621.7	4,006.3	40.48	6.5	16.4	1.90	NA	1.09	4.06	NA	NA
Regency Centers Corp (REG)	65.13	6,453.2	2,021.4	8,474.6	23.85	4.9	21.7	2.56	2.19	1.94	2.98	50.61	128.7
Retail Opportunity Investment Corp. (ROIC)	17.37	1,615.3	743.4	2,358.6	31.52	6.8	21.7	0.97	NA	0.68	3.91	NA	NA
Ramco-Gershenson Properties Trust (RPT)	18.81	1,598.1	923.5	2,521.6	36.63	6.3	17.4	1.16	0.82	0.80	4.25	17.14	109.7

(continued)

Table 14. US REIT Comparative Analysis, as of 13 March 2015 (continued)

Sector/Company (Ticker)	Price (USD)	Total Equity Market Cap (USD millions)	Total Debt (USD millions)	Total Market Value (USD millions)	Debt to Total Market Value	Net Debt to Recurring EBITDA	EV/Recurring EBITDA	2013 FFO per Share	2013 CAD per Share	Indicated Dividend	Dividend Yield	Barclays NAV	Price/Barclays NAV
Retail: shopping centre (continued)													
Urstadt Biddle (UBA)	22.61	791.6	306.3	1,098.0	27.90%	5.0×	18.2×	0.97	NA	1.02	4.51%	NA	NA
Weingarten Realty Investors (WRI)	35.32	4,529.0	1,938.2	6,467.2	29.97	5.5	18.7	1.93	1.34	1.38	3.91	27.24	129.7%
Retail: shopping centre total/weighted average		63,614.6	31,502.8	95,117.3	33.12%	6.4×	21.2×				3.45%		124.0%
Specialty													
EPR Properties (EPR)	59.06	3,708.7	1,645.5	5,354.2	30.73%	4.8×	15.7×	3.91	NA	3.63	6.15%	NA	NA
Getty Realty Corp. (GTY)	17.80	594.8	125.3	720.2	17.40	2.3	13.6	1.31	NA	0.88	4.94	NA	NA
Plum Creek Timber Company, Inc. (PCL)	42.23	7,428.3	3,298.0	10,726.3	30.75	5.4	18.0	NA	NA	1.76	4.17	NA	NA
Rayonier (RYN)	26.96	3,409.5	751.6	4,161.1	18.06	3.7	25.2	NA	NA	1.00	3.71	NA	NA
Specialty total/weighted average		15,141.3	5,820.4	20,961.7	27.77%	4.8×	18.9×				4.58%		NA
Storage													
CubeSmart (CUBE)	23.29	3,946.0	1,173.9	5,119.8	22.93%	5.4×	23.8×	0.90	0.65	0.64	2.75%	15.58	149.5%

(continued)

Table 14.   US REIT Comparative Analysis, as of 13 March 2015 (continued)

Sector/ Company (Ticker)	Price (USD)	Total Equity Market Cap (USD millions)	Total Debt (USD millions)	Total Market Value (USD millions)	Debt to Total Market Value	Net Debt to Recurring EBITDA	EV/ Recurring EBITDA	2013 FFO per Share	2013 CAD per Share	Indicated Dividend	Dividend Yield	Barclays NAV	Price/ Barclays NAV
Storage (continued)													
Extra Space Storage (EXR)	64.92	7,837.5	2,369.9	10,207.4	23.22%	5.6×	24.5×	2.01	1.55	1.88	2.90%	34.92	185.9%
Public Storage (PSA)	188.23	36,828.1	64.4	36,892.5	0.17	(0.1)	21.7	7.53	7.18	5.60	2.98	128.58	146.4
Sovran Self Storage (SSS)	90.49	3,100.3	801.1	3,901.4	20.53	4.3	21.3	3.72	2.79	3.00	3.32	69.90	129.5
Storage total/ weighted average		51,711.9	4,409.2	56,121.2	7.86%	1.5×	22.3×				2.97%		151.6%
Student housing													
American Campus Communities (ACC)	41.34	4,479.4	2,972.7	7,452.1	39.89%	7.0×	17.6×	2.20	1.72	1.52	3.68%	40.58	101.9%
Campus Crest Communities (CCG)	7.74	647.3	618.4	1,265.7	48.86	504.3	1045.5	0.82	0.80	0.36	4.65	7.15	108.3
Education Realty Trust (EDR)	34.84	1,684.3	711.1	2,395.4	29.69	5.2	17.9	1.64	1.22	1.44	4.13	11.13	313.0
Student housing total/ weighted average		6,811.0	4,302.3	11,113.2	38.71%	53.8×	115.4×		1.51	1.39	3.88%	30.12	154.7%

(continued)

Table 14. US REIT Comparative Analysis, as of 13 March 2015 (continued)

Sector/Company (Ticker)	Price (USD)	Total Equity Market Cap (USD millions)	Total Debt (USD millions)	Total Market Value (USD millions)	Debt to Total Market Value	Net Debt to Recurring EBITDA	EV/Recurring EBITDA	2013 FFO per Share	2013 CAD per Share	Indicated Dividend	Dividend Yield	Barclays NAV	Price/Barclays NAV
Technology													
CoreSite Realty Corp. (COR)	47.30	1,139.7	318.5	1,458.2	21.84%	2.2×	10.4×	1.82	NA	1.68	3.55%	NA	NA
DuPont Fabros Technology (DFT)	32.40	2,979.3	1,025.0	4,004.3	25.60	3.8	15.3	1.46	1.73	1.68	5.19	37.98	85.3%
Digital Realty (DLR)	64.95	10,052.8	4,673.1	14,725.9	31.73	4.5	14.3	5.14	3.88	3.40	5.23	67.56	96.1
Technology total/weighted average		14,171.8	6,016.6	20,188.5	29.80%	4.2×	14.2×				5.09%		93.7%
Overall total/weighted average		774,837.6	366,524.4	1,141,362.1	32.11%	6.2×	21.3×				3.40%		115.3%

Note: EV is enterprise value, NM is not meaningful, and NA is not available.
Sources: Based on Barclays Research estimates and data from Thomson Reuters, Bloomberg, SNL Financial, and First Call.

Table 15. European REITs as of 9 March 2015

Company	Ticker	Currency	Price	Total Market Cap (local currency, millions)	Total Debt (local currency, millions)	Loan to Value	EV/ Recurring EBITDA	Cash Flow per Share	Indicated Dividend	Dividend Yield	Last Reported NAV	Price/NAV
Big Yellow Group PLC	BYG LN	GBP	645.5	971	238	28.0%	30.4	20.7	16.4	2.54%	420.5	53.52%
British Land	BLND LN	GBP	839.5	8,414	4,891	40.0	26.7	28.6	27.0	3.22	688.1	22.01
Capital & Counties Properties PLC	CAPC LN	GBP	408.5	3,349	585	9.2	125.8	1.6	1.5	0.37	310.7	31.48
Capital & Regional	CAL LN	GBP	56.75	399	354	53.0	39.8	2.9	2.9	5.11	59.5	–4.61
Intu Properties plc	INTU LN	GBP	348	4,518	4,643	44.4	24.7	13.3	13.7	3.94	378.6	–8.09
Derwent London	DLN LN	GBP	3,405	3,719	1,013	28.0	43.9	55.9	39.7	1.16	2801.3	21.55
Development Securities PLC	DSC LN	GBP	245.5	294	155	44.7	43.5	–1.2	4.8	1.95	268.5	–8.58
Grainger plc	GRI LN	GBP	207.7	857	1,179	46.5	123.4	21.2	2.5	1.20	239.2	–13.18%
Great Portland Estates plc	GPOR LN	GBP	807.5	2,750	1,059	25.7	86.0	6.3	8.7	1.08	568.7	42.00
Hammerson	HMSO LN	GBP	667.5	5,188	2,259	38.0	28.4	23.9	20.4	3.06	629.5	6.03
Helical Bar plc	HLCL LN	GBP	390.5	465	397	46.0	–421.9	–23.7	6.1	1.56	312.6	24.93
Land Securities	LAND LN	GBP	1,265	9,795	4,204	32.5	27.6	37.0	30.7	2.43	1012.7	24.91

(continued)

Table 15. European REITs as of 9 March 2015 (continued)

Company	Ticker	Currency	Price	Total Market Cap (local currency, millions)	Total Debt (local currency, millions)	Loan to Value	EV/ Recurring EBITDA	Cash Flow per Share	Indicated Dividend	Dividend Yield	Last Reported NAV	Price/NAV
LondonMetric Property plc	LMP LN	GBP	161.9	999	332	31.6%	27.6	4.2	7.0	4.32%	121.0	33.76%
Quintain plc	QED LN	GBP	98.75	508	252	23.0	-549.3	-1.7	0.0	0.00	114.5	-13.76
SEGRO	SGRO LN	GBP	427.5	3,168	2,040	43.6	25.5	16.4	15.1	3.53	360.4	18.63
Shaftesbury plc	SHB LN	GBP	816	2,216	611	23.6	43.0	12.2	13.6	1.67	712.6	14.51
St. Modwen Properties	SMP LN	GBP	462.9	994	379	35.0	78.5	25.7	4.0	0.86	343.8	34.64
UNITE Group	UTG LN	GBP	553.5	1,118	697	48.0	21.5	15.1	11.2	2.02	417.6	32.53
Workspace Group	WKP LN	GBP	850	1,345	343	31.0	44.5	13.1	9.8	1.16	495.5	71.54
alstria	AOX GR	GBP	12.162	951	817	52.0	21.7	0.6	0.5	4.11	11.0	10.65
Beni Stabili	BNS IM	EUR	0.7405	1,674	2,212	53.0	21.5	0.0	0.0	2.97	0.9	-15.29
Citycon	CTY1S FH	EUR	3.12	1,822	1,143	36.7	19.8	0.2	0.2	4.81	3.0	3.27
Cofinimmo	COFB BB	EUR	107.2	1,920	1,604	48.9	21.8	5.8	5.5	5.13	96.1	11.57
Deutsche Annington	ANN GY	EUR	32.58	8,763	6,101	50.9	33.6	1.1	0.7	2.14	21.3	52.63

(continued)

Table 15. European REITs as of 9 March 2015 (continued)

Company	Ticker	Currency	Price	Total Market Cap (local currency, millions)	Total Debt (local currency, millions)	Loan to Value	EV/ Recurring EBITDA	Cash Flow per Share	Indicated Dividend	Dividend Yield	Last Reported NAV	Price/NAV
Deutsche EuroShop	DEQ GY	EUR	44.295	2,368	1,374	43.0%	21.1	2.0	1.3	2.93%	32.8	35.23%
Eurocommercial Properties	ECMPA NA	EUR	41.25	1,778	1,088	42.0	21.1	2.0	1.9	4.70	35.7	15.50
Foncière des Régions	FDR FP	EUR	87.81	5,795	4,962	50.8	22.6	5.0	4.2	4.78	75.5	16.27
Gecina	GFC FP	EUR	116.85	7,377	3,881	38.0	24.1	5.2	4.7	3.98	106.8	9.38
Grand City Properties	GYC GY	EUR	15.15	1,748	667	38.9	45.1	0.4	0.0	0.00	6.9	119.56
Icade	ICAD FP	EUR	78.07	5,707	3,809	42.3	18.2	4.3	3.7	4.78	78.4	−0.41
Klépierre	LI FP	EUR	43.455	13,055	5,491	40.9	27.6	2.1	1.6	3.68	32.1	35.50
LEG Immobilien	LEG GY	EUR	70.79	3,984	2,778	47.7	29.6	2.1	1.8	2.59	53.3	32.86
PSP Swiss	PSPN SW	EUR	92.35	4,211	1,906	28.1	25.7	3.8	3.3	3.52	102.1	−9.59
TLG	TLG GY	EUR	15.84	930	487	0.0	—	0.0	0.0	0.00	17.6	−9.84
Unibail-Rodamco	UL NA	EUR	253.35	24,429	12,157	41.1	23.7	9.9	9.6	3.79	167.2	51.52
Vastned	VASTN NA	EUR	44.15	855	589	44.6	18.8	2.4	2.0	4.53	42.7	3.45
Wereldhave	WHA NA	EUR	62.32	2,137	1,132	31.6	31.9	3.0	2.9	4.61	54.4	14.66

Note: EV is enterprise value.
Sources: Based on J.P. Morgan Cazenove estimates and data from Company Reports and DataStream.

INDUSTRY RESOURCES

- Asian Public Real Estate Association (APREA)

  APREA is a non-profit industry association that represents and promotes the real estate asset class in the Asia-Pacific region. It is the industry body for the suppliers and users of capital in the real estate sector.

  www.aprea.asia

- National Association of Real Estate Investment Trusts (NAREIT)

  NAREIT is the worldwide representative voice for REITs and publicly traded real estate companies with an interest in US real estate and capital markets. NAREIT's members are REITs and other businesses throughout the world that own, operate, and finance income-producing real estate, as well as those firms and individuals who advise, study, and service those businesses.

  www.reit.com

- European Public Real Estate Association (EPRA)

  As a member of REESA (Real Estate Equity Securitization Alliance), EPRA works in close coordination with NAREIT in the United States, APREA in Asia, and other industry organisations to promote common interests in this dynamic international industry. EPRA strives to establish best practices in accounting, reporting, and corporate governance; to provide high-quality information to investors; and to create a framework for debate and decision making on the issues that determine the future of the sector. On many issues, EPRA works in unison globally with sister associations.

  www.epra.com

- British Property Federation

  The British Property Federation is a membership organisation devoted to representing the interests of all those involved in real estate ownership and investment.

  www.bpf.org.uk

■ Property Council of Australia

The Property Council of Australia is the leading advocate for Australia's AUD600 billion property industry. It counts the bulk of the nation's major investors, property owners, and developers, as well as the industry's professional service and trade providers, among its members. The organisation is governed by a board comprising key leaders from the industry.

www.propertyoz.com.au

■ Real Property Association of Canada (REALpac)

REALpac is Canada's most senior, influential, and informative voice in the real property investment industry. REALpac brings together the industry's chief executives to collectively influence public policy, to educate government and the public, to ensure stable and beneficial real estate property and capital markets, and to promote the performance of the real property sector in Canada.

www.realpac.ca

■ Real Estate Equity Securitization Alliance (REESA)

REESA is a global alliance to further equity investment in real estate on a securitised basis. REESA focuses on cross-border investment, international taxation, financial reporting standards initiatives, and educational outreach to investors. The members of REESA are leading member-based trade associations with a significant interest in the world of securitised equity real estate investment.

www.ares.or.jp

INDUSTRY JOURNALS

■ *Journal of Property Research*

The *Journal of Property Research* is an international journal of research, particularly applied research, into property investment and development.

www.tandfonline.com/action/journalInformation?show=aimsScope&journalCode=RJPR20#.VAN-e_ldX3M

- *Journal of Property Investment & Finance*

  The *Journal of Property Investment & Finance* is an international forum for the interchange of information and ideas relating to property valuation and investment, property management, and decision making in the commercial property market. The aim is to inform and encourage debate internationally between academics and practising professionals in all aspects of real estate research and practice.

  www.emeraldgrouppublishing.com/products/journals/journals.htm?id=JPIF

- *REIT Magazine* (Real Estate Investment Today)

  http://mediakits.theygsgroup.com/nareit-2014/reit-magazine/reit-magazine

EVENTS AND CONFERENCES

- REIT Symposium by New York University School of Professional Studies

  www.scps.nyu.edu/academics/departments/schack/conferences-events/reit-symposium.html

- EPRA Annual Conference

  www.epra.com/networking-and-events/epra-annual-conference-2014/

- REITWorld, REITWeek, and REITWise: NAREIT's Law, Accounting & Finance Conferences

  NAREIT's Law, Accounting & Finance Conferences provide attendees with a broad yet focused educational programme that presents a clear picture of current political, economic, and market events that impact legal, financial, and accounting operations within REITs and publicly traded real estate companies.

  www.reit.com/nareit/events/reitwise

  www.reit.com/nareit/events/reitworld

  www.reit.com/nareit/events/reitweek

- Bank of America Merrill Lynch Australian REIT Annual Conference

- JP Morgan Asia Pacific Real Estate Conference

- JP Morgan Australian REITs 1x1 Forum

Made in the USA
Middletown, DE
05 January 2017